KB087144

GRAMMAR
101

Level 1

Grammar 101 Level 1

지은이 넥서스영어교육연구소
펴낸이 임상진
펴낸곳 (주)넥서스

출판신고 1992년 4월 3일 제311-2002-2호 2-8
10880 경기도 파주시 지목로 5
Tel (02)330-5500 Fax (02)330-5555

ISBN 979-11-6165-135-4 54740
　　　979-11-6165-142-2 (SET)

www.nexusbook.com

※ 본 책은 워크북을 추가하고, After School Grammar의 콘텐츠를 재구성한 것입니다.

한번에 끝내는
중등 영문법

GRAMMAR

101

넥서스영어교육연구소 지음

Level 1

NEXUS Edu

GRAMMAR 101 is...

basic
'기초 과정의, 입문의, 기본의'라는 뜻의 Grammar 101 [wʌ́nouwʌ́n]으로
영문법 기초를 최단 기간에 마스터할 수 있도록 구성하였습니다.

easy
예비 중부터 누구나 쉽게 단계별로 공부할 수 있습니다.
Level 1~3까지는 중학교 과정을 쉽게 마스터할 수 있도록 구성되어 있습니다.

rich
각 Lesson의 Practice뿐만 아니라 워크북에서도 내신에 자주 등장하는
다양하고 풍부한 단답형, 서술형 문제를 제공합니다.

useful
문법뿐만 아니라 실용적인 다양한 표현을 배웁니다.
실생활에서 사용할 수 있는 실용적인 표현들을 엄선하여 예문에 활용했습니다.

systematic
체계적으로 공부할 수 있도록 구성하였습니다.
시험에 나올 수 있는 문제들을 체계적이고 반복적으로 학습하면서
문법의 원리와 규칙들을 자연스럽게 습득합니다.

confident
내신시험에 자신감을 심어줍니다.
문법을 알기 쉽게 설명하고 있으며, 각 학년에서 다루는 문법만을
집중적으로 공부함으로써 내신시험에 보다 효과적으로대비할 수 있습니다.

up to date
최신 기출문제 유형을 제공합니다.
전국 중학교에서 출제된 문법문제들을 각 학년별로 분석하여,
최신 문제 유형을 미리 학습할 수 있으며,
서술형 문제를 더욱 보충하여 내신시험에 대비할 수 있도록 했습니다.

1 Grammar Lesson

중요 핵심 문법을 빠르게 이해하고, 기억하기
쉽도록 도표, 도식, 그림을 이용하였습니다.
내신에 꼭 필요한 사항만을 담아, 최단기간에
각 단계별 영문법을 마스터할 수 있도록 구성
하였습니다.

2 Practice

다양한 유형의 풍부한 문제 풀이를 통해 내신
대비는 물론, 영어의 4가지 영역(L, R, S, W)
을 공부하는 기초를 습득할 수 있습니다. 문제
를 풀면서 자신의 취약점을 확인하고, 단계별
문제를 통해 기초부터 심화까지 학습할 수 있
습니다.

3 VOCA in Grammar

문법 문제 속에 있는 어휘를 찾아 앞에서 배운
기초 문법을 한 번 더 쉽게 확인할 수 있습니다.
어휘의 영영풀이를 통해 어휘의 개념뿐만 아니
라 문법의 기초 개념까지도 파악할 수 있도록
구성하였습니다.

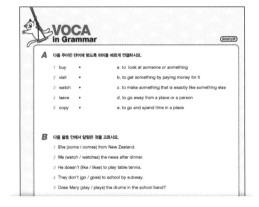

4 Workbook

각 레슨별로 최신 기출 문제 유형을 담아 다양한 문제풀이를 할 수 있도록 구성하였습니다. 각 Lesson 및 Practice 학습 후, 자기주도학습으로 워크북을 활용할 수 있도록 구성하였습니다.

5 Chapter Review

철저한 내신 분석을 통해 기출과 유사한 시험 문제를 풀어볼 수 있도록 시험지 형태로 구성하였습니다. 챕터 안에서 배웠던 문법 사항들을 통합하여 학습할 수 있도록 하였습니다.

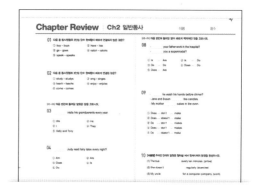

추가 제공 자료(www.nexusbook.com)

어휘 리스트
& 테스트지

통문장 영작
테스트지

통문장 해석
테스트지

동사 · 비교급 변화표
& 테스트지

문법
용어집

모바일단어장
추가 제공

이 책의 차례

CONTENTS

✏ **Chapter 1** be동사와 인칭대명사

1 be동사　　　　　　　　　　　　008
　be동사의 과거형
2 be동사의 부정문　　　　　　　　010
　be동사의 Yes/No 의문문
3 인칭대명사　　　　　　　　　　012
4 There is[are]　　　　　　　　　014
　How many

　VOCA in Grammar　　　　　　016

✏ **Chapter 2** 일반동사

1 일반동사　　　　　　　　　　　018
　일반동사의 현재형
2 일반동사의 부정문　　　　　　　020
　일반동사의 의문문

　VOCA in Grammar　　　　　　022

✏ **Chapter 3** 시제

1 과거시제　　　　　　　　　　　024
2 현재시제 vs. 과거시제　　　　　026
3 진행시제　　　　　　　　　　　028

　VOCA in Grammar　　　　　　030

✏ **Chapter 4** 조동사

1 can　　　　　　　　　　　　　032
　may
2 must　　　　　　　　　　　　034
　should
3 will, be going to　　　　　　　036

　VOCA in Grammar　　　　　　038

✏ **Chapter 5** 명사와 대명사

1 명사　　　　　　　　　　　　　040
2 관사　　　　　　　　　　　　　042
3 지시대명사　　　　　　　　　　044
　부정대명사 one
　all, each, every
4 비인칭 주어 it　　　　　　　　　046
　비인칭 주어 it vs. 인칭대명사 it

　VOCA in Grammar　　　　　　048

✏️ Chapter 6 형용사/부사/비교

1 형용사   050
2 부사   052
3 비교급/최상급의 형태   054
   비교급/최상급 구문

   VOCA in Grammar   056

✏️ Chapter 7 to부정사와 동명사

1 to부정사   058
2 동명사   060
3 to부정사와 동명사   062
   동사원형을 목적격보어로 취하는 동사
   to부정사와 동명사의 관용 표현

   VOCA in Grammar   064

✏️ Chapter 8 문장의 형태

1 문장의 구성요소   066
   1형식
   2형식
2 3형식   068
   4형식
   5형식

   VOCA in Grammar   070

✏️ Chapter 9 문장의 종류

1 명령문   072
   제안문
2 감탄문   074
3 부가의문문   076
4 의문사가 있는 의문문   078

   VOCA in Grammar   080

✏️ Chapter 10 접속사와 전치사

1 등위접속사   082
2 종속접속사   084
3 시간을 나타내는 전치사   086
4 장소를 나타내는 전치사   088

   VOCA in Grammar   090

✏️ Workbook

✏️ Chapter Review

LEVEL 2 CONTENTS

Chapter 1 시제
1 진행시제
2 현재완료
  현재완료의 형태
  현재완료와 과거시제
3 현재완료의 용법

Chapter 2 조동사
1 can / could
  may / might
  will / would
2 must
  should / ought to
3 had better
  used to
  would like to
  would rather

Chapter 3 수동태
1 능동태와 수동태
  수동태의 여러 가지 형태
2 수동태의 시제
  조동사가 있는 수동태
  「by+행위자」의 생략

Chapter 4 to부정사
1 명사적 용법
2 형용사적 용법
  부사적 용법
3 가주어와 진주어
  to부정사의 의미상의 주어
  to부정사의 관용 표현

Chapter 5 동명사
1 동명사의 역할
2 동명사와 to부정사
3 분사
  동명사 vs. 현재분사

Chapter 6 명사와 대명사
1 가산명사와 불가산명사
  물질명사의 수량 표현
2 명사의 소유격
  재귀대명사
3 부정대명사 Ⅰ
4 부정대명사 Ⅱ

Chapter 7 형용사와 부사 & 비교
1 주의해야 할 형용사
2 주의해야 할 부사
3 원급 비교
  비교급
4 최상급
  관용 표현

Chapter 8 가정법
1 가정법 과거
2 가정법 if vs. 조건의 if
  I wish 가정법 과거

Chapter 9 관계사
1 관계대명사
  주격 관계대명사
2 목적격 관계대명사
  소유격 관계대명사
  관계대명사의 생략
3 관계부사

Chapter 10 접속사
1 시간을 나타내는 접속사
  이유를 나타내는 접속사
2 조건을 나타내는 접속사
  양보를 나타내는 접속사
3 상관접속사
  명사절을 이끄는 접속사 that

LEVEL 3 CONTENTS

Chapter 1 부정사
1 명사적 역할
  형용사적 역할
  부사적 역할
2 to부정사의 의미상의 주어
  to부정사의 시제
  to부정사의 태
3 to부정사 vs. 동명사
4 목적격보어로 쓰이는 to부정사, 원형부정사
  관용 표현

Chapter 2 분사와 분사구문
1 분사의 종류
  분사의 쓰임
  현재분사와 동명사의 구별
2 분사구문
3 분사구문의 시제와 태
  관용 표현

Chapter 3 완료시제
1 현재완료
  현재완료 vs. 과거
  현재완료진행
  현재완료 vs. 현재완료진행
2 과거완료
  과거완료와 과거
  과거완료진행

Chapter 4 수동태
1 수동태의 의미와 형태
2 4문형의 수동태
  5문형의 수동태
3 주의해야 할 수동태

Chapter 5 조동사
1 used to 관련 표현
  can 관련 표현
  may 관련 표현
2 조동사+have+과거분사

Chapter 6 비교
1 비교급을 이용한 표현
2 원급을 이용한 표현
3 최상급을 이용한 표현

Chapter 7 가정법
1 가정법 과거
  단순 조건 vs. 가정법 과거
  가정법 과거완료
  혼합가정법
2 I wish 가정법
  as if 가정법
  without, but for 가정법

Chapter 8 관계사
1 관계대명사
  주격 관계대명사
  목적격 관계대명사
  소유격 관계대명사
2 한정적 용법 vs. 계속적 용법
  관계대명사 that, what
  관계대명사 that vs. 접속사 that
3 관계부사
4 복합관계사

Chapter 9 접속사
1 명사절을 이끄는 접속사 that
  명사절을 이끄는 접속사 whether/if
2 의문사가 있는 간접의문문
  의문사가 없는 간접의문문
3 부사절을 이끄는 접속사 Ⅰ〈시간, 조건〉
4 부사절을 이끄는 접속사 Ⅱ〈이유, 양보〉

Chapter 10 화법, 강조, 도치, 일치
1 화법 / 평서문의 화법 전환
  화법 전환 시의 시제 변화
2 의문사가 있는 의문문의 화법 전환
  의문사가 없는 의문문의 화법 전환
  명령문의 화법 전환
3 강조 / 도치
4 시제 일치 / 시제 일치의 예외
  수의 일치

Chapter
01
be동사와 인칭대명사

Lesson 1 be동사 be동사의 과거형
Lesson 2 be동사의 부정문 be동사의 Yes/No 의문문
Lesson 3 인칭대명사
Lesson 4 There is[are] ~. How many ~?

Grammar
Lesson 1

★ be동사

❶ be동사(am/are/is) ~이다 / ~에 있다

I am a lawyer. 나는 변호사이다.

You are a bright student. 너는 총명한 학생이다.

Anna is in the park. Anna는 공원에 있다.

❷ 주어가 인칭대명사일 경우, 「주어+be동사」는 줄여 쓸 수 있다.

인칭		주어	be동사	축약형		인칭	주어	be동사	축약형
단수	1	I	am	I'm	복수	1	we		we're
	2	you	are	you're		2	you	are	you're
	3	he	is	he's		3	they		they're
		she		she's					
		it		it's					

I am [I'm] a pretty girl. 나는 예쁜 소녀이다.

She is [She's] in the classroom. 그녀는 교실에 있다.

They are [They're] good friends. 그들은 좋은 친구들이다.

★ be동사의 과거형

be동사의 과거형 (was/were) ~가 이었다' 또는 '~에 있었다

인칭		주어	과거형		인칭	주어	과거형
단수	1	I	was	복수	1	we	
	2	you	were		2	you	were
	3	he			3	they	
		she	was				
		it					

* 주로 과거를 나타내는 부사(구) yesterday, last ~, ~ ago, then 등과 함께 쓴다.

I was in Canada last year. 나는 작년에 캐나다에 있었다.

He was absent from school yesterday. 그는 어제 학교에 결석했다.

We were happy at that time. 그때 우리는 행복했다.

They were at the playground two hours ago. 그들은 두 시간 전에 운동장에 있었다.

Practice

Answers p.02

A 다음 빈칸에 am, are, is 중 알맞은 것을 써 넣으시오.

1 I _____ a football player.

2 Jeju _____ an island.

3 You _____ my best friend.

4 Her uncle _____ in Paris now.

5 Jeremy and I _____ in the hospital.

6 Sally and her family _____ on vacation.

Hint

you and I	= we
Jake and I	
he and she	= they
Kevin and Meg	
you and she	= you
you and Ben	

B 다음 빈칸에 알맞은 be동사의 과거형을 써 넣으시오.

1 Jake _____ in Mexico in 2016.

2 I _____ afraid of dogs at that time.

3 We _____ at the library last weekend.

4 She _____ busy yesterday, but she is free now.

5 Bill and Andrew _____ in the same class last year.

6 You and your brother _____ good at swimming two weeks ago.

C 다음 괄호 안의 대명사를 주어로 하는 문장으로 다시 쓰시오. (단, 축약된 부분은 축약형으로 쓸 것)

1 He's from New York. (You) → _____

2 I'm thirteen years old. (We) → _____

3 We're hungry and tired. (I) → _____

4 They were in the kitchen. (He) → _____

5 She was sick yesterday. (They) → _____

6 Ben was sad at that time. (We) → _____

Eng-Eng VOCA

football	a game played with an oval ball which players kick, throw, or carry
island	a piece of land surrounded by water
hospital	a building where sick people receive medical treatment
afraid	feeling fear
hungry	wanting to eat something

Grammar
Lesson 2

❶ 현재형의 부정문: am/are/is+not ~가 아니다, ~에 없다

I <u>am</u> good at math. 나는 수학을 잘한다.

I <u>am not</u> good at math. 나는 수학을 잘 못한다.
= I'm not good at math.

We are not[aren't] in the same grade. 우리는 같은 학년이 아니다.
It is not[isn't] his car. 그것은 그의 차가 아니다.

❷ 과거형의 부정문: was/were+not ~가 아니었다, ~에 없었다

The movie was not[wasn't] interesting. 그 영화는 재미가 없었다.
You were not[weren't] at home yesterday. 너는 어제 집에 있지 않았다.

❶ 현재형의 의문문: Am/Are/Is+주어 ~? ~이니?, ~에 있니?

<u>You</u> <u>are</u> a middle school student. 너는 중학생이다.

<u>Are</u> <u>you</u> a middle school student? 너는 중학생이니?

Is your car blue? 너의 자동차는 파란색이니?
Are they really angry? 그들은 정말로 화가 났니?

❷ 과거형의 의문문: Was/Were+주어 ~? ~였니?, ~에 있었니?

A: Was your exam difficult? 시험이 어려웠니?
B: Yes, it was. / No, it wasn't. 네, 어려웠어요. / 아니요, 어렵지 않았어요.

A: Were they late again? 그들이 또 늦었나요?
B: Yes, they were. / No, they weren't. 네, 늦었어요. / 아니요, 늦지 않았어요.

❸ 의문문에 대한 응답: Yes, 주어+be동사. / No, 주어+be동사+not.

A: Is Alice a fashion designer? Alice는 패션 디자이너인가요?
B: Yes, she is. / No, she isn't. 네, 맞아요. / 아니요, 아니에요.

A: Are you baseball players? 당신들은 야구 선수인가요?
B: Yes, we are. / No, we aren't. 네, 맞아요. / 아니요, 아니에요.

A: Was your brother sick yesterday? 어제 네 남동생이 아팠니?
B: Yes, he was. / No, he wasn't. 네, 아팠어요. / 아니요, 아프지 않았어요.

Practice

A 다음 문장을 부정문과 의문문으로 바꿔 쓰시오.

> **Plus**
> 「be동사+not」은 줄여 쓸 수 있지만, am not은 줄여 쓸 수 없다.
> It isn't my car. (O)
> 그것은 내 차가 아니다.
> I amn't a doctor. (X)

1 She's in the car.

부정문 → _____

의문문 → _____

2 He was busy yesterday.

부정문 → _____

의문문 → _____

3 You and your brother are twins.

부정문 → _____

의문문 → _____

4 They were at the shopping mall last weekend.

부정문 → _____

의문문 → _____

B 다음 밑줄 친 부분을 어법에 맞게 고쳐 쓰시오.

1 <u>Is</u> Cindy and Andrew American?

2 Derek and I <u>am not</u> from Germany.

3 <u>Were</u> Miranda a singer in the band?

4 He <u>are not</u> smart and funny.

C 다음 빈칸에 알맞은 말을 넣어 대화를 완성하시오.

> **Hint**
> 의문문에 답할 경우 주어는 대명사로 쓰여야 한다.
> A: Is Mr. Harvey there?
>   Harvey 씨가 거기에 계신가요?
> B: Yes, he is.
>   네, 계세요.

1 A: _____ _____ ready for the final test?

B: Yes, I am.

2 A: _____ _____ a good concert?

B: Yes, it was. The band was excellent!

3 A: David, are you Canadian?

B: _____, _____ _____. I'm British.

4 A: Is your father a firefighter?

B: _____, _____ _____. He is a scientist.

Eng-Eng VOCA

twin	one of two children born at the same time to the same mother
singer	a person who sings, or whose job is singing
funny	making you laugh
excellent	very good
firefighter	a person whose job is to put out fires

Grammar
Lesson 3

모바일단어장

★ 인칭대명사

▷ 인칭대명사의 격 변화

단·복수	인칭	주격	소유격	목적격	소유대명사
단수	1	I	my	me	mine
	2	you	your	you	yours
	3	he	his	him	his
		she	her	her	hers
		it	its	it	—
복수	1	we	our	us	ours
	2	you	your	you	yours
	3	they	their	them	theirs

* 인칭대명사는 사람이나 사물을 대신하여 쓰는 대명사로, '나'를 말하는 1인칭, '너'를 말하는 2인칭, '나, 너를 제외한 나머지'를 말하는 3인칭이 있다.

❶ 주격(~은, 는, 이, 가): 문장에서 주어 역할을 한다.

I am good at tennis. 나는 테니스를 잘 친다.
She is a new science teacher. 그녀는 새로 온 과학 선생님이시다.
They are from the United States. 그들은 미국에서 왔다.

❷ 소유격(~의): 명사 앞에 쓰인다.

My boyfriend is a famous football player. 내 남자 친구는 유명한 미식축구 선수이다.
Your notebook is on the sofa. 너의 공책은 소파 위에 있다.
We live with **our** grandmother. 우리는 할머니와 함께 산다.

❸ 목적격(~을, 를, 에게): 문장에서 목적어 역할을 한다.

My grandparents love **me** very much. 조부모님은 나를 매우 사랑하신다.
Mr. Brown teaches **us** history. Brown 선생님은 우리에게 역사를 가르치신다.
I visited **them** in Beijing. 나는 베이징으로 그들을 방문했다.

❹ 소유대명사(~의 것): 「소유격+명사」를 대신한다.

This yellow raincoat is **mine**. 이 노란색 비옷은 나의 것이다.
That old umbrella is **his**. 저 낡은 우산은 그의 것이다.
These albums are **theirs**. 이 앨범들은 그들의 것이다.

Practice

Answers p.03

A 다음 괄호 안에서 알맞은 것을 고르시오.

1 That dress is pretty. I want to buy (it / his / them).

2 Look at the flowers! (It / We / They) are very beautiful.

3 Jane is from England. (His / Her / Their) family is in London.

4 Joe and Ally went to the mall. (You / We / They) like shopping.

B 다음 밑줄 친 부분을 알맞은 인칭대명사로 바꿔 쓰시오.

its는 it의 소유격이고, it's는 it is의 축약형이다.

1 Alex and Sherry love comic books.

→ _____ love comic books.

2 I like Andrew, but Andrew likes Kathy.

→ I like _____, but _____ likes Kathy.

3 Jessica plays tennis with her friends.

→ _____ plays tennis with her friends.

4 My grandfather has an armchair. The armchair is very old.

→ My grandfather has an armchair. _____ is very old.

5 I have a rabbit. The rabbit's ears are very long.

→ I have a rabbit. _____ ears are very long.

C 다음 〈보기〉와 같이 문장을 완성하시오.

소유격은 단독으로 쓰이지 않고 뒤에 반드시 명사가 와야 하지만, 소유대명사는 단독으로 쓰인다.

This is my camera.
(소유격) 이것은 내 카메라이다.

This camera is mine.
(소유대명사) 이 카메라는 내 것이다.

> 보기   It's my cell phone. The cell phone is _____mine_____.

1 That is their car. The car is _____.

2 It's your uniform. The uniform is _____.

3 These are her mittens. The mittens are _____.

4 They're his sunglasses. The sunglasses are _____.

5 This is our house. The house is _____.

Eng-Eng VOCA

history	the story of past events; events of the past
comic book	a book that tells stories through pictures
armchair	a comfortable chair with sides that you can rest your arms on
uniform	a special kind of clothing that is worn by all the members of a group or organization
mitten	a covering for the hand that has a separate part for the thumb only

Grammar
Lesson 4

★ There is[are] ~.

❶ 긍정문: There is+단수명사 / There are+복수명사 ~(들)이 있다

There is <u>a banana</u> in my bag. 내 가방에 바나나가 한 개 있다.

There are <u>some trees</u> in the garden. 정원에 나무가 몇 그루 있다.

There are <u>six puppies</u> in the box. 상자 안에 강아지 여섯 마리가 있다.

* 「There is[are] ~.」 구문의 주어는 be동사 뒤에 있는 명사이다. 이 경우, There는 해석하지 않는다.

❷ 부정문: There is[are]+not ~. ~(들)이 없다

There is not[isn't] a museum in my hometown. 내 고향에는 박물관이 없다.

There are not[aren't] any comic books in the library. 도서관에는 만화책이 없다.

There are not[aren't] any banks around here. 이 주변에는 은행이 없다.

❸ 의문문: Is[Are] there ~?

A: Is there a drugstore near your house? 당신의 집 근처에 약국이 있나요?

B: Yes, there is. 네, 있어요.

A: Was there a swimming pool in the hotel? 그 호텔에 수영장이 있었나요?

B: No, there wasn't. 아니요, 없었어요.

A: Are there three apples in the basket? 바구니에 사과 세 개가 있나요?

B: No, there aren't. There is only one apple. 아니요, 단 한 개 있어요.

* 의문문에 대한 응답은 「Yes, there is[are].」 또는 「No, there isn't[aren't].」로 한다.

★ How many ~?

How many ~ are there? ~가 몇 개 있니?

A: How many erasers are there on the desk? 책상 위에 지우개가 몇 개 있니?

B: There are five erasers on the desk. 책상 위에 지우개가 다섯 개 있어.

A: How many oranges are there in your hands? 네 손에 오렌지가 몇 개 있니?

B: There are two oranges in my hands. 내 손에 오렌지가 두 개 있어.

Practice

Answers p.03

A 다음 괄호 안에서 알맞은 것을 고르시오.

1 There (is / are) a building near the park.

2 There (is / are) many horses on the farm.

3 There (is / are) a pretty girl under the tree.

4 There (is / are) two hundred students at our school.

> **Plus**
>
> there가 장소를 나타내는 부사일 경우 '거기에, 그곳에'라고 해석한다.
>
> A: We often go there.
> 우리는 그곳에 자주 간다.
>
> B: Who's that man over there?
> 저기에 있는 저 남자는 누구니?

B 다음 문장을 부정문과 의문문으로 바꿔 쓰시오.

1 There is a mirror in the classroom.

부정문 → _____

의문문 → _____

2 There are many rivers in Brazil.

부정문 → _____

의문문 → _____

3 There are fifty students in the library.

부정문 → _____

의문문 → _____

4 There is a chocolate cake on the table.

부정문 → _____

의문문 → _____

C 다음 대화의 빈칸에 알맞은 말을 쓰시오.

1 A: _____ _____ a pineapple?

B: Yes, there is. Just a moment, please.

2 A: Is there a red pen?

B: No, _____ _____. I only have pencils.

3 A: How _____ elephants are there in the zoo?

B: _____ _____ eleven elephants in the zoo.

4 A: _____ _____ many computers in your classroom?

B: Yes, there are. We use them for class.

Eng-Eng VOCA

farm	a piece of land used for growing crops or raising animals
mirror	a piece of glass that reflects images
library	a building where books, newspapers, videos, and music are kept for people to read, use, or borrow
moment	a very short period of time
zoo	a place where wild animals are kept for people to see

VOCA in Grammar

Answers p.03

A 다음 주어진 단어에 맞도록 의미를 바르게 연결하시오.

1 lawyer •   a. a particular level of job

2 playground •   b. someone whose job is to advise people about laws

3 grade •   c. a place for children to play

4 raincoat •   d. a shop where you can buy medicines

5 drugstore •   e. a coat that you wear to protect yourself from rain

B 다음 괄호 안에서 알맞은 것을 고르시오.

1 You (is / are) a bright student.

2 They (was / were) at the playground two hours ago.

3 There (is / are) a banana in my bag.

4 There (is / are) not any banks around here.

5 How many oranges (is / are) there in your hands?

C 다음 〈보기〉에서 알맞은 단어를 골라 문장을 완성하시오.

| 보기 | our   she   they   us   mine |

1 _____ is a new science teacher.

2 We live with _____ grandmother.

3 Mr. Brown teaches _____ history.

4 This yellow raincoat is _____.

5 _____ are from the United States.

Chapter
02
일반동사

Lesson 1 일반동사 ★ 일반동사의 현재형
Lesson 2 일반동사의 부정문 ★ 일반동사의 의문문

Grammar
Lesson 1

★ 일반동사

be동사	am, are, is, was, were
조동사	can, may, will, must, should ...
일반동사	go, leave, study, like, eat ...

* 일반동사는 be동사와 조동사를 제외한 모든 동사로, 주어의 동작이나 상태를 나타낸다.

We go to school by bike. 우리는 자전거를 타고 학교에 간다.

Jenny leaves for work at 6:00 a.m. Jenny는 오전 여섯 시에 직장으로 떠난다.

★ 일반동사의 현재형

대부분의 동사	+ -s	speaks, visits, loves, likes, cleans, comes, eats, runs, reads, helps, sings ...
-o, -x, -s, -ss, -sh, -ch로 끝나는 동사	+ -es	does, goes, washes, watches, teaches, passes, catches, fixes, mixes, kisses ...
「자음+y」로 끝나는 동사	-y → -ies	study → studies fly → flies try → tries copy → copies cry → cries
「모음+y」로 끝나는 동사	+ -s	says, plays, buys, enjoys ...
불규칙동사	have	has

* 일반동사의 현재형은 주어가 3인칭 단수인 경우를 제외하고 모두 동사원형을 쓴다.
주어가 3인칭 단수일 경우, 동사원형에 -s나 -es를 붙인다.

I come from Australia. 나는 호주 출신이다.

She comes from New Zealand. 그녀는 뉴질랜드 출신이다.

We watch the news after dinner. 우리는 저녁 식사 후에 뉴스를 본다.

My mom watches a soap opera after dinner. 우리 엄마는 저녁 식사 후에 드라마를 보신다.

They study Chinese every day. 그들은 매일 중국어를 공부한다.

Uncle Tom studies Korean every day. Tom 삼촌은 매일 한국어를 공부하신다.

Their children play the guitar. 그들의 자녀는 기타를 연주한다.

He plays tennis with his brother. 그는 남동생과 테니스를 친다.

You have a nice smartphone. 너는 좋은 스마트폰을 가지고 있다.

Kate has a brand-new tablet PC. Kate는 새로 나온 태블릿 PC를 가지고 있다.

Practice

A 다음 괄호 안에서 알맞은 것을 고르시오.

1 Joe (like / likes) hip-hop music.

2 Miranda (miss / misses) her aunt.

3 My grandfather (love / loves) me.

4 I (talk / talks) to Victoria about our homework.

5 She (brush / brushes) her hair in the morning.

6 Emma and Julia (take / takes) a walk every day.

7 Many people (worry / worries) about their health.

B 다음 괄호 안의 주어진 동사를 현재형으로 바꿔 문장을 완성하시오.

1 We _____ for him in the office. (wait)

2 He _____ a surprise party. (enjoy)

3 I _____ a picture on a canvas. (draw)

4 You _____ a pretty teddy bear. (have)

5 Mrs. White _____ math at the university. (teach)

6 Ashley and David _____ Spanish very well. (speak)

7 My grandmother _____ a newspaper in the morning. (read)

C 다음 괄호 안의 대명사를 주어로 하는 문장으로 고쳐 쓰시오.

1 He wears black jeans. (they)

→ _____

2 I eat a peanut butter sandwich. (Mike)

→ _____

3 Joy and Sophia have brown hair. (my sister)

→ _____

4 She sits in the first row in class. (he and I)

→ _____

Eng-Eng VOCA	
miss	to feel sad because you can no longer see someone or do something
worry	to keep thinking about bad things that might happen
university	a place where students study at a high level to get a degree
newspaper	a set of paper sheets containing news, articles, and advertisements
row	a line of things or people next to each other

Grammar
Lesson 2

★ 일반동사의 부정문

I, we, you, they ... (1인칭, 2인칭, 3인칭 복수 주어)	do not [don't] + 동사원형
she, he, it ... (3인칭 단수 주어)	does not [doesn't] + 동사원형

We **know** the answer. 우리는 답을 안다.

→ We **do not**[**don't**] **know** the answer. 우리는 답을 모른다.

She **likes** tomato spaghetti. 그녀는 토마토 스파게티를 좋아한다.

→ She **does not**[**doesn't**] **like** tomato spaghetti. 그녀는 토마토 스파게티를 좋아하지 않는다.

I **do not**[**don't**] **speak** Japanese. 나는 일본어를 못한다.

They **do not**[**don't**] **go** to school by subway. 그들은 지하철을 타고 학교에 가지 않는다.

He **does not**[**doesn't**] **like** to play table tennis. 그는 탁구 치는 것을 좋아하지 않는다.

Her sister **does not**[**doesn't**] **wear** skirts. 그녀의 여동생은 치마를 입지 않는다.

★ 일반동사의 의문문

I, we, you, they ... (1인칭, 2인칭, 3인칭 복수 주어)	Do + 주어 + 동사원형 ~? – Yes, 주어 + do. / No, 주어 + don't.
she, he, it ... (3인칭 단수 주어)	Does + 주어 + 동사원형 ~? – Yes, 주어 + does. / No, 주어 + doesn't.

You **study** math every night. 너는 매일 밤 수학을 공부한다.

→ **Do** you **study** math every night? 너는 매일 밤 수학을 공부하니?

He **lives** in Toronto with his family. 그는 가족과 함께 토론토에 산다.

→ **Does** he **live** in Toronto with his family? 그는 가족과 함께 토론토에 사니?

A: **Do** you **take** a shower in the morning? 너는 아침에 샤워를 하니?

B: **Yes, I do.** 응, 그래.

A: **Does** your brother **have** a car? 너의 형은 차가 있니?

B: **Yes, he does.** He has a small car. 네, 있어요. 그는 작은 차를 가지고 있어요.

A: **Does** Mary **play** the drums in the school band? Mary는 학교 밴드에서 드럼을 연주하니?

B: **No, she doesn't.** She plays the guitar in the school band.

아니요, 그녀는 드럼을 연주하지 않아요. 그녀는 학교 밴드에서 기타를 연주해요.

Grammar
Lesson 3

「be동사＋-ing」의 형태로 특정 시점에서 진행 중인 일을 나타내며, 시제에 따라 현재진행, 과거진행, 미래진행으로 나뉜다.

❶ -ing형 만들기

대부분의 경우	＋-ing	walking, looking, watching, crying, reading
-e로 끝나는 동사	-e를 빼고＋-ing	living, coming, making, writing, giving
-ie로 끝나는 경우	-ie → -y＋-ing	die → dying　　　　lie → lying tie → tying
「단모음＋단자음」으로 끝나는 경우	마지막 자음을 한번 더 쓰고＋-ing	sit → sitting　　　cut → cutting stop → stopping　swim → swimming

❷ 현재진행(~하고 있다, ~하는 중이다)

She **is walking** in the park. 그녀는 공원을 걷고 있다.

They **are building** a house in their hometown. 그들은 자신의 고향에서 집을 짓고 있다.

* 현재 진행 중인 동작을 나타낸다.

❸ 과거진행((과거에) ~하고 있었다, ~하는 중이었다)

My sister **was writing** a postcard. 내 여동생은 엽서를 쓰고 있었다.

We **were having** lunch together. 우리는 함께 점심을 먹고 있었다.

* 과거의 어느 한 시점에서 일시적으로 진행된 동작이나 상태를 나타낸다.

❹ 진행시제의 부정문과 의문문

▷ 부정문: be동사＋not＋-ing

I **am not waiting** for Peter. 나는 Peter를 기다리고 있지 않다.

Mom, David **is not cleaning** his room now. 엄마, 지금 David는 방 청소를 하고 있지 않아요.

She **was not singing** a song at that time. 그녀는 그때 노래를 부르고 있지 않았다.

We **were not learning** Yoga at the gym then. 우리는 그때 체육관에서 요가를 배우고 있지 않았다.

▷ 의문문: be동사＋주어＋-ing ~?

A: **Is** your brother **studying** for the exam? 당신의 남동생은 시험공부를 하고 있나요?

B: No, he isn't. He **is playing** computer games. 아니요, 그는 컴퓨터 게임을 하고 있어요.

A: **Were** you **playing** the drums at 10 p.m. yesterday? 어젯밤 열 시에 드럼을 치고 있었나요?

B: No, I wasn't. I **was taking** a bath then. 아니요, 저는 그때 목욕하고 있었어요.

* 진행시제의 의문문에 대한 응답은 「Yes, 주어＋be동사.」 또는 「No, 주어＋be동사＋not.」로 한다.

Practice

Answers p.04

A 다음 괄호 안에서 알맞은 것을 고르시오.

1 She doesn't (walk / walks) very fast.

2 I (don't / doesn't) have enough money.

3 Does he really (like / likes) card games?

4 Natalie (don't / doesn't) like hamburgers.

5 (Do / Does) Joe and Jake write English poems?

> **plus**
>
> 일반동사의 부정문과 의문문을 만드는 조동사 do는 해석하지 않지만, 일반동사 do는 '~을 하다'라고 해석한다.
>
> (조동사)
> I don't drink coffee at night.
> 나는 밤에 커피를 마시지 않는다.
>
> (일반동사)
> Sue does her homework at home.
> Sue는 집에서 숙제를 한다.

B 다음 문장을 부정문과 의문문으로 바꿔 쓰시오.

1 This dress looks good.

부정문 → _____

의문문 → _____

2 Sophia has lots of hobbies.

부정문 → _____

의문문 → _____

3 You wear white sneakers.

부정문 → _____

의문문 → _____

4 George brings his lunch to school every day.

부정문 → _____

의문문 → _____

C 다음 주어진 동사를 현재형으로 하여 대화를 완성하시오.

1 A: _____ Chris _____(study) English every day?

B: No, _____ _____.

2 A: _____ you _____(know) Helen?

B: Yes, _____ _____. We are very close friends.

3 A: _____ they _____(have) a map of Rome?

B: Yes, _____ _____. They're ready for the trip.

> **Eng-Eng VOCA**
>
> | | |
> |---|---|
> | enough | as many/much as someone needs |
> | poem | a piece of writing that expresses emotions and ideas in short lines |
> | hobby | an activity that you enjoy doing in your free time |
> | bring | to come to a place with someone/something |
> | map | a picture that shows the rivers, mountains, and streets in an area |

VOCA
in Grammar

Answers p.05

A 다음 주어진 단어에 맞도록 의미를 바르게 연결하시오.

1 buy •

2 visit •

3 watch •

4 leave •

5 copy •

a. to look at someone or something

b. to get something by paying money for it

c. to make something that is exactly like something else

d. to go away from a place or a person

e. to go and spend time in a place

B 다음 괄호 안에서 알맞은 것을 고르시오.

1 She (come / comes) from New Zealand.

2 We (watch / watches) the news after dinner.

3 He doesn't (like / likes) to play table tennis.

4 They don't (go / goes) to school by subway.

5 Does Mary (play / plays) the drums in the school band?

C 다음 〈보기〉에서 알맞은 단어를 골라 문장을 완성하시오.

| 보기 | studies | know | live | wear | has |

1 Mark _____ in-line skates.

2 He _____ math every night.

3 We don't _____ the answer.

4 My sister doesn't _____ skirts.

5 Does he _____ in Toronto with his family?

Chapter
03
시제

Lesson 1 과거시제
Lesson 2 현재시제 vs. 과거시제
Lesson 3 진행시제

Grammar
Lesson 1

모바일단어장

★ 과거시제

❶ 일반동사의 과거형: 규칙 변화 동사와 불규칙 변화 동사가 있다.

▷ 규칙 변화 동사

대부분의 동사	+ -ed	wanted, talked, opened, called, started, helped, visited	
-e로 끝나는 동사	+ -d	hated, loved, invited, liked, moved	
「자음+y」로 끝나는 동사	-y → -ied	study → studied carry → carried try → tried	cry → cried worry → worried
「모음+y」로 끝나는 동사	+ -ed	played, enjoyed	
「단모음+단자음」으로 끝나는 동사	자음을 한번 더 쓰고 + -ed	stop → stopped drop → dropped	plan → planned prefer → preferred

* 동사의 과거형은 현재형과 달리 주어의 인칭이나 수의 영향을 받지 않는다.

Eric called me last night. Eric이 어젯밤에 내게 전화했다.

The beautiful girl danced with her father. 아름다운 소녀가 아버지와 춤을 추었다.

▷ 불규칙 변화 동사

begin – began	give – gave	lend – lent	sleep – slept	cost – cost
break – broke	go – went	lose – lost	speak – spoke	cut – cut
buy – bought	grow – grew	make – made	spend – spent	hit – hit
come – came	have – had	meet – met	steal – stole	hurt – hurt
do – did	hear – heard	run – ran	teach – taught	put – put
drink – drank	keep – kept	say – said	tell – told	read – read
find – found	know – knew	sing – sang	think – thought	[ri:d] – [red]
get – got	leave – left	sit – sat	write – wrote	

They went to the amusement park last week. 그들은 지난주에 놀이공원에 갔다.

I hurt my leg yesterday. 나는 어제 다리를 다쳤다.

❷ 과거시제의 부정문: did not[didn't] + 동사원형

Jake didn't pass the driving test. Jake는 운전면허 시험에 합격하지 못 했다.

They didn't buy birthday presents for Julia. 그들은 Julia에게 줄 생일 선물을 사지 않았다.

❸ 과거시제의 의문문: Did + 주어 + 동사원형 ~?

Sandy waited for Jane. Sandy가 Jane을 기다렸다.

→ **Did Sandy wait for Jane?** Sandy가 Jane을 기다렸니?

A: **Did you have a good vacation?** 즐거운 휴가를 보냈나요?

B: **Yes, I did. I had a fun time.** 네, 그래요. 저는 즐거운 시간을 보냈어요.

* 과거시제의 의문문에 대한 응답은 「Yes, 주어+did.」 또는 「No, 주어+didn't.」로 한다.

Practice

Answers p.05

A 다음 괄호 안의 동사를 과거형으로 바꿔 문장을 완성하시오.

1 I _____ a letter to my sister. (send)

2 Kate _____ the meat with a knife. (cut)

3 Diana _____ Japanese at school. (learn)

4 She _____ her cell phone in her car. (find)

5 The grocery store _____ yesterday. (open)

6 He _____ to the United States last year. (go)

B 다음 문장을 괄호 안의 지시대로 고쳐 쓰시오.

1 He didn't see me. (긍정문)

  → _____

2 They saw *Superman* last weekend. (의문문)

  → _____

3 We went to Central Park yesterday morning. (부정문)

  → _____

4 Jeremy lost his digital camera yesterday. (의문문)

  → _____

5 The children broke the window by mistake. (부정문)

  → _____

C 다음 괄호 안의 동사를 이용하여 대화를 완성하시오.

1 (leave) A: _____ Sarah _____ for home already?

       B: Yes, she did. She _____ an hour ago.

2 (sell) A: _____ you _____ your old house in Seoul?

       B: Yes, I did. I _____ it three months ago.

3 (make) A: _____ Sally _____ a sandcastle at the beach?

       B: No, she didn't. She _____ a necklace with seashells.

Eng-Eng VOCA

knife	a sharp blade with a handle that is used for cutting
grocery store	a store that sells food and other things used in the home
mistake	something you do that is not sensible or has a bad result
already	before now
necklace	a piece of jewelry to wear around the neck

Grammar
Lesson 2

모바일단어장

★ 현재시제 vs. 과거시제

과거   현재   미래

① 현재시제

▷ 변하지 않는 진리나 일반적인 사실, 반복적인 행동이나 습관, 현재의 상태를 나타낼 때, 현재시제를 쓴다.

The Earth goes around the Sun. (진리 · 사실) 지구는 태양 주위를 돈다.

I eat breakfast at seven o'clock every day. (반복적인 행동 · 습관) 나는 매일 일곱 시에 아침을 먹는다.

Sunny reads books in the library after school. (반복적인 행동 · 습관) Sunny는 방과 후에 도서관에서 책을 읽는다.

Billy looks happy now. (현재의 상태) Billy는 지금 행복해 보인다.

▷ go, come, leave, arrive, end, start 등의 동사는 이미 확정된 미래의 일을 의미할 때 현재시제를 쓰기도 한다.

The airplane for London leaves at 10 a.m. 런던으로 가는 비행기는 오전 열 시에 떠난다.

The festival starts this Saturday night. 축제는 이번 토요일 밤에 시작한다.

② 과거시제

▷ 이미 끝난 과거의 동작이나 상태를 나타낼 때, 과거시제를 쓴다.

Kelly went to the museum last Sunday. Kelly는 지난 일요일에 박물관에 갔다.

Tracy was a high school student at that time. Tracy는 그때 고등학생이었다.

▷ 역사적 사실을 설명할 때는 과거시제로 쓴다.

Columbus reached America in 1492. 콜럼버스는 1492년에 아메리카 대륙에 도착했다.

The Second World War broke out in 1939. 제2차 세계 대전은 1939년에 일어났다.

▷ 과거시제는 주로 과거를 나타내는 부사(구)와 함께 쓴다.

> yesterday, then, at that time, last night[week, month, year], ~ ago ...

Chris lost his car key last week. Chris는 지난주에 자동차 열쇠를 잃어버렸다.

They ate dinner an hour ago. 그들은 한 시간 전에 저녁을 먹었다.

Practice

Answers p.06

A 다음 괄호 안에서 알맞은 것을 고르시오.

현재시제는 every day, every Saturday, once a week [month, year], on Sundays 등과 같은 부사구와 함께 쓰이기도 한다.

My grandmother goes to church on Sundays.
할머니는 일요일마다 교회에 가신다.

I play baseball with my friends every day.
나는 친구들과 함께 매일 야구를 한다.

1 He (has / had) a nightmare last night.

2 She (is / was) fifteen years old this year.

3 I (eat / ate) a ham sandwich an hour ago.

4 Ben flew to Egypt (tomorrow / last weekend).

5 Jasmine (brushes / brushed) her teeth ten minutes ago.

B 다음 표의 내용과 일치하도록 빈칸에 알맞은 말을 쓰시오.

	yesterday	every day
Rachel	study English	chat on the Internet
Nick	read comic books	play computer games
Andrew	visit grandparents	go swimming

1 Nick _____ comic books yesterday.

2 Andrew _____ swimming every day.

3 Rachel _____ English yesterday.

4 Every day Nick _____ computer games.

C 다음 우리말과 같은 뜻이 되도록 주어진 단어를 배열하여 문장을 완성하시오.

1 개구리는 겨울에 잠을 잔다. (sleep, during the winter, frogs)

→ _____

2 그 영화는 오후 열 시에 시작한다. (starts, the movie, at 10 p.m.)

→ _____

3 나는 한 시간 전에 그림 그리는 것을 끝마쳤다. (the picture, finished, an hour ago, I)

→ _____

4 그들은 어젯밤에 그 축구 경기를 봤다. (last night, watched, they, the soccer game)

→ _____

Eng-Eng VOCA

nightmare	a very bad dream
fly	to travel by plane
chat	to talk to someone in a friendly, informal way
visit	to go and spend time in a place or with someone
sleep	to rest your mind and body by closing your eyes

Practice

Answers p.06

A 다음 주어진 동사의 진행형을 이용하여 문장을 완성하시오.

1 I _____ my room at that time. (clean)

2 I saw Jane. She _____ on the phone. (talk)

3 Five people _____ on the bench now. (sit)

4 Please be quiet! The baby _____ now. (sleep)

5 The children _____ in the river an hour ago. (swim)

B 다음 문장을 괄호 안의 지시대로 고쳐 쓰시오.

> **Hint**
> have가 '~을 먹다'라는 뜻일 경우 진행형이 가능하지만, '~을 가지고 있다'라는 뜻일 경우 진행형으로 쓸 수 없다.
> I <u>am having</u> bacon and eggs for breakfast.
> 나는 아침 식사로 베이컨과 달걀을 먹고 있다.
> She <u>has</u> many pretty rings and earrings.
> 그녀는 예쁜 반지와 귀걸이를 많이 가지고 있다.

1 They were riding horses on the farm. (부정문으로)

→ _____

2 He was looking for his wallet this morning. (의문문으로)

→ _____

3 Sue is reading a newspaper on the couch. (의문문으로)

→ _____

4 We are having lunch now. (부정문으로)

→ _____

C 다음 우리말과 같은 뜻이 되도록 괄호 안의 주어진 단어를 이용하여 문장을 완성하시오.

1 나는 그때 책을 읽고 있었다. (read)

→ I _____ a book then.

2 그녀는 공원에서 자전거를 타고 있다. (ride)

→ She _____ a bike in the park.

3 Henry는 지금 낮잠을 자고 있다. (take a nap)

→ Henry _____ now.

4 그들은 그때 소파에 앉아 있었다. (sit)

→ They _____ on the sofa then.

Eng-Eng VOCA

quiet	making very little noise
river	a natural flow of water that goes into the sea
look for	to try to find something or someone
wallet	a small case that holds things (such as money and credit cards)
nap	a short sleep, especially during the day

VOCA
in Grammar

Answers p.06

A 다음 주어진 단어에 맞도록 의미를 바르게 연결하시오.

1 steal   •   a. to start doing something

2 hurt   •   b. to let someone borrow money for a short time

3 grow   •   c. to take something that belongs to someone else

4 begin   •   d. to feel pain in part of your body

5 lend   •   e. to become bigger and taller

B 다음 괄호 안에서 알맞은 것을 고르시오.

1 They (go / went) to the amusement park lask week.

2 She (hurt / hurts) her leg yesterday.

3 We (eat / ate) breakfast at seven o'clock every day.

4 Did Sandy (wait / waited) for Jane last night?

5 Jake didn't (pass / passed) the driving test.

C 다음 〈보기〉에서 알맞은 단어를 골라 문장을 완성하시오.

> **보기**   writing   building   learning   taking   having

1 We were _____ lunch together then.

2 She wasn't _____ Yoga at the gym then.

3 They are _____ a house in their hometown.

4 I was _____ a bath then.

5 My sister is _____ a postcard now.

Chapter

04

조동사

Lesson 1 can may
Lesson 2 must should
Lesson 3 will, be going to

Grammar
Lesson 1

❶ 능력이나 가능: ~할 수 있다(= be able to)

▷ **긍정문: can + 동사원형**

I can speak Spanish very well. 나는 스페인어를 매우 잘 말할 수 있다.

= **I am able to speak** Spanish very well.

Jason can run very fast. Jason은 매우 빨리 달릴 수 있다.

▷ **부정문: cannot [can't] + 동사원형**

Andrew **cannot [can't] play** the flute. Andrew는 플루트를 연주할 수 없다.

We **can't tell** Anna the truth. 우리는 Anna에게 진실을 말할 수가 없다.

▷ **의문문: Can + 주어 + 동사원형 ~?**

<u>You</u> <u>can</u> <u>swim</u> in the river.

<u>Can</u> <u>you</u> <u>swim</u> in the river? 너는 강에서 수영할 수 있니?

A: **Can he ride** a bicycle? 그는 자전거를 탈 수 있니?

B: **Yes, he can. / No, he can't.** 응, 탈 수 있어. / 아니, 탈 수 없어.

* 의문문에 대한 응답은 「Yes, 주어+can.」 또는 「No, 주어+can't.」로 한다.

❷ 허가: ~해도 된다(= may)

You **can borrow** my tennis racket. 너는 내 테니스 라켓을 빌려가도 좋다.

Can I use your digital camera? 내가 네 디지털 카메라를 사용해도 될까?

❸ 「Can/Could you ~?」는 상대방에게 도움을 요청하거나 부탁할 때 쓰기도 한다.

Can you turn on the computer? 컴퓨터를 켜 줄래?

Could you close the door, please? 문 좀 닫아주시겠어요?

❶ 허가: ~해도 된다(= can)

You **may eat** ice cream after lunch. 너는 점심 식사 후에 아이스크림을 먹어도 좋다.

You **may not sit** here. 너는 여기에 앉아서는 안 된다.

May I stay here? 제가 이곳에 머물러도 될까요?

❷ 추측: ~일지도 모른다

My father **may go** fishing this Friday. 아버지는 이번 주 금요일에 낚시하러 갈지도 모른다.

Mike **may not come** to the meeting. Mike는 회의에 오지 않을지도 모른다.

Practice

Answers p.07

A 다음 밑줄 친 조동사의 의미를 〈보기〉에서 골라 그 기호를 쓰시오.

> **보기** (a) 능력 (b) 허가 (c) 추측

1 You <u>can</u> leave now. _____

2 My father <u>can</u> play the violin. _____

3 They <u>may</u> not remember your name. _____

4 Angela <u>may</u> bring some cookies for us. _____

5 <u>May</u> I borrow your notebook after school? _____

6 Jason <u>can</u> speak both English and French. _____

B 다음 주어진 문장을 괄호 안의 지시대로 고쳐 쓰시오.

1 He may pass the exam. (부정문)

→ _____

2 She can speak German fluently. (be able to 긍정문)

→ _____

3 They can swim in the pool all night. (부정문)

→ _____

4 We can see monkeys and tigers in the zoo. (의문문)

→ _____

> **plus**
> 요청이나 부탁, 허가에 대한 답변
>
> ◈ 승낙할 때
> · Yes, you may[can].
> · Of course.
> · No problem.
> · Sure.
>
> ◈ 거절할 때
> · No, you may not.
> · Sorry, you can't.
> · I'm afraid not.

C 다음 밑줄 친 부분을 어법에 맞게 고쳐 쓰시오.

1 My sister can <u>dances</u> a tango.

2 She <u>wasn't able to made</u> pasta.

3 May I <u>asks</u> your phone number?

4 Is she able <u>pass</u> the math exam?

5 I <u>can call not</u> you on Saturday night.

6 Can you <u>gave</u> this dictionary to me?

> **plus**
> can은 다른 조동사와 함께 쓸 때 be able to로 써야 한다.
>
> He will be able to go to school tomorrow.
> 그는 내일 학교에 갈 수 있을 것이다.

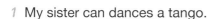

Eng-Eng VOCA

remember	to keep some information in your mind
fluently	with an ability to express oneself easily
pool	an area of water to swim in
exam	a test to show someone's knowledge or ability
dictionary	a book that gives a list of words and explains their meanings

Grammar
Lesson 2

모바일단어장

★ must

❶ 필요나 의무

▷ must[have to]+동사원형 '~해야 한다'

You must finish your report today. 너는 오늘 보고서를 끝내야 한다.

=You have to finish your report today.

It's so late. We have to go home now. 너무 늦었어. 우리는 지금 집에 가야만 해.

All drivers must wear seat belts. 모든 운전자는 안전벨트를 매야 한다.

▷ must not vs. don't have to

강한 금지	must not+동사원형: ~해서는 안 된다
불필요	don't[doesn't] have to+동사원형: ~할 필요가 없다

You must not make a noise in the library. 너는 도서관에서 떠들어서는 안 된다.

You must not tell a lie. 너는 거짓말을 해서는 안 된다.

I can hear you. You don't have to shout. 나는 네 소리를 들을 수 있다. 너는 소리 지를 필요가 없다.

Today is a holiday. He doesn't have to work. 오늘은 휴일이다. 그는 일할 필요가 없다.

▷ 조동사 must는 과거형이 없으므로, have to의 과거형 had to를 쓴다.

I got up late. I had to take a taxi. 나는 늦게 일어났다. 나는 택시를 타야만 했다.

We had to go there. 우리는 그곳에 가야만 했다.

❷ 강한 추측 '~임에 틀림없다'

She has a nice car. She must be rich. 그녀는 좋은 차를 가지고 있다. 그녀는 부자임이 틀림없다.

Brian is absent from school. He must be sick. Brian은 학교에 결석했다. 그는 아픈 것이 틀림없다.

★ should 의무, 당연, 충고

❶ 긍정문: should+동사원형 '~해야 한다, ~하는 것이 좋겠다'

You should eat more fruits and vegetables. 너는 과일과 채소를 더 많이 먹어야 한다.

You should take a rest. 너는 휴식을 취해야 한다.

❷ 부정문: should not[shouldn't]+동사원형

You shouldn't eat too much fast food. 너는 패스트푸드를 너무 많이 먹지 않아야 한다.

You shouldn't drive so fast. 너는 운전을 그렇게 빨리 하지 않아야 한다.

❸ 의문문: Should+주어+동사원형 ~?

A: Should I trust Justin? 내가 Justin을 믿어야 하나요?

B: Yes, you should. / No, you shouldn't. 네, 그래야 해요. / 아니요, 그러면 안돼요.

Practice

A 다음 밑줄 친 조동사의 의미를 〈보기〉에서 골라 그 기호를 쓰시오.

> **보기**　　(a) 의무, 충고　　(b) 금지　　(c) 강한 추측　　(d) 불필요

1 You <u>must</u> not park here.　　_____

2 We <u>must</u> clean our classroom.　　_____

3 He didn't sleep last night. He <u>must</u> be tired.　　_____

4 You have a fever. You <u>must</u> go to see a doctor.　　_____

5 We <u>don't have to</u> hurry. We have a lot of time.　　_____

6 Young children <u>should</u> swim with their parents.　　_____

B 다음 우리말과 같은 뜻이 되도록 괄호 안에서 알맞은 것을 고르시오.

1 나는 오늘 밤에 그녀에게 전화해야 한다.

　→ I (should / should not) call her tonight.

2 그 영화는 틀림없이 재미있을 것이다.

　→ The movie (must / has to) be interesting.

3 너는 다시는 지각해서는 안 된다.

　→ You (must not / don't have to) be late again.

4 Edward는 안경을 쓸 필요가 없다.

　→ Edward (must not / doesn't have to) wear glasses.

> **plus**
>
> 의무를 나타내는 의문문은 「Must+주어+동사원형~?」 또는 「Do[Does]+주어+have to+동사원형~?」을 쓴다.
>
> <u>Must</u> I wait for him?
> = <u>Do</u> I have to wait for him?
> 내가 그를 기다려야만 하나요?

C 다음 밑줄 친 부분을 어법에 맞게 고쳐 쓰시오.

1 She must <u>goes</u> to bed early.

2 You <u>should are</u> kind to old people.

3 Children must not <u>saw</u> this movie.

4 Kate and Tom <u>has to</u> work late tonight.

5 He doesn't have to <u>washes</u> the dishes.

6 You <u>should eat not</u> too much junk food.

park	to put a car in a place for a period of time
fever	a body temperature that is higher than normal
hurry	to do something or go somewhere more quickly than usual
call	to contact or try to contact a person by phone
junk food	unhealthy food with a lot of fat and sugar

Grammar
Lesson 3

★ will, be going to

❶ will '~할 것이다, ~하겠다'

▷ 「will + 동사원형」은 미래의 일이나 주어의 의지를 나타낸다.

I will be fourteen years old next year. (미래) 나는 내년에 열네 살이 될 것이다.
It will rain tomorrow. (미래) 내일은 비가 올 것이다.
Your bag looks heavy. I will help you. (주어의 의지) 네 가방은 무거워 보여. 내가 너를 도와줄게.

▷ 부정문: will not[won't] + 동사원형

Becky will not[won't] be busy this week. Becky는 이번 주에 바쁘지 않을 것이다.
I won't change my schedule. 나는 내 일정을 변경하지 않을 것이다.

▷ 의문문: Will + 주어 + 동사원형 ~?

A: Will she come to the party? 그녀가 파티에 올 거니?
B: Yes, she will. 응, 올 거야.

A: Will they go to the movies tonight? 그들이 오늘 밤에 영화 보러 갈 거니?
B: No, they will not[won't]. 아니, 안 갈 거야.

* 의문문에 대한 응답은 「Yes, 주어+will.」 또는 「No, 주어+will not[won't].」로 한다.

❷ be going to '~할 것이다, ~할 예정이다'

▷ 「be going to + 동사원형」은 가까운 미래의 일이나 계획을 나타낸다.

The airplane is going to arrive in Beijing soon. (가까운 미래의 일) 비행기가 곧 베이징에 도착할 것이다.
He is going to play soccer this afternoon. (계획) 그는 오늘 오후에 축구를 할 것이다.

▷ 부정문: be동사 + not + going to + 동사원형

I'm not going to travel to Greece this summer. 나는 이번 여름에 그리스로 여행을 가지 않을 것이다.
She is not going to come here today. 그녀는 오늘 이곳에 오지 않을 것이다.

▷ 의문문: Be동사 + 주어 + going to + 동사원형 ~?

A: Are you going to call her? 그녀에게 전화할 거니?
B: Yes, I am. 응, 전화할 거야.

A: Is he going to play basketball tomorrow? 그는 내일 농구할 거니?
B: No, he isn't. 아니, 하지 않을 거야.

* 의문문에 대한 응답은 「Yes, 주어+be동사.」 또는 「No, 주어+be동사+not.」로 한다.

Practice

Answers p.07

A 다음 괄호 안에서 알맞은 것을 고르시오.

1 (Are / Will) you be there tonight?

2 Tony will (be / is) a famous actor someday.

3 Jack (isn't / won't) going to climb the mountain.

4 (Is / Are) Emma going to call us next weekend?

5 I'm going to (help / helps) my mother with shopping.

6 We missed the train. We (take / will take) the next one.

B 다음 문장을 괄호 안의 지시대로 바꿔 쓰시오.

1 I met him last weekend. (be going to 긍정문)

→ _____ this weekend.

2 Ben went to the gallery yesterday. (will 긍정문)

→ _____ tomorrow.

3 She is going to drink coffee after lunch. (be going to 부정문)

→ _____ after lunch.

4 Linda is going to move to a new house next month. (be going to 의문문)

→ _____ next month?

5 My uncle will play baseball with his friends next Sunday. (will 부정문)

→ _____ next Sunday.

> **Plus**
>
> 'Will/Would you ~?」는 '~해 줄래(요)?'라는 뜻으로, 상대방에게 도움을 요청하거나 부탁하는 표현이다.
>
> Will you help me?
> 나 좀 도와줄래?
> Would you help me, please?
> 저를 좀 도와주시겠어요? (더 정중한 표현)

C 다음 주어진 동사를 이용하여 대화를 완성하시오.

1 A: _____ Samantha _____ (be) at school today?

   B: No, she won't. She broke her arm two days ago.

2 A: _____ Alice _____ _____ _____ (leave) for London?

   B: Yes, she is. She is going to leave tomorrow.

3 A: _____ they _____ _____ _____ (clean) the classroom after school?

   B: No, they aren't. They're going to clean the gym.

> **Eng-Eng VOCA**
>
> famous   known to many people
> actor   a person who acts in a play or movie
> climb   to go up mountains, cliffs, etc., as a sport
> gallery   a room or building for showing paintings or sculptures
> break   to make something separate into two or more pieces

VOCA
in Grammar

Answers p.08

A 다음 주어진 단어에 맞도록 의미를 바르게 연결하시오.

1 absent •
2 holiday •
3 shout •
4 arrive •
5 travel •

a. a time of rest from work and school
b. not at school, work or meeting
c. to get to the place you are going to
d. to go from one place to another
e. to say something very loudly

B 다음 괄호 안에서 알맞은 것을 고르시오.

1 Andrew (can / is able) to play the flute.

2 Can he (ride / rides) a bicycle?

3 I will (be / am) fourteen years old next year.

4 Will she (come / coming) to the party?

5 The airplane is (going to / will) arrive in Beijing soon.

C 다음 〈보기〉에서 알맞은 단어를 골라 문장을 완성하시오.

| 보기 | must | go | tell | had to | eat |

1 You don't have to _____ a lie.

2 You should _____ more fruits and vegetables.

3 You _____ finish your report today.

4 I _____ take a taxi yesterday.

5 My father may _____ fishing this Friday.

Chapter
05

명사와 대명사

Lesson 1 명사
Lesson 2 관사
Lesson 3 지시대명사   부정대명사 one   all, each, every
Lesson 4 비인칭 주어 it   비인칭 주어 it vs. 인칭대명사

Grammar
Lesson 1

★ **명사** 사람이나 동·식물, 사물, 장소의 이름이나 보이지 않는 추상적인 개념 등을 나타내는 말

❶ 셀 수 있는 명사: 주로 –(e)s를 붙여 복수형을 만든다.

▷ 셀 수 있는 명사의 복수형

대부분의 명사	+ -s	pencils, girls, maps, stars, books, cars, desks, students, schools ...
-s, -x, -ch, -sh로 끝나는 명사	+ -es	buses, classes, benches, dishes, boxes, foxes ...
「자음+y」로 끝나는 명사	y → -ies	baby → babies city → cities party → parties lady → ladies factory → factories ※ 「모음+y」로 끝나는 명사+ -s: boys, toys, keys ...
「자음+o」로 끝나는 명사	+ -es	heroes, potatoes, tomatoes ... ※ 예외: pianos, photos
-f(e)로 끝나는 명사	f(e) → -ves	knife → knives leaf → leaves life → lives thief → thieves wife → wives wolf → wolves
불규칙한 복수형		man → men woman → women foot → feet child → children mouse → mice tooth → teeth goose → geese
단·복수의 형태가 같은 명사		sheep, fish, deer ...

I have one **car**, and she has three **cars**. 나는 차가 한 대 있고, 그녀는 차가 세 대 있다.

Two **leaves** fell on the floor. 나뭇잎 두 개가 바닥에 떨어졌다.

Many **children** are playing soccer in the playground. 많은 어린이들이 운동장에서 축구를 하고 있다.

My grandfather has twelve **deer**. 할아버지는 사슴 열두 마리를 가지고 계신다.

❷ 셀 수 없는 명사: 단수형으로 쓰고, 단수 취급을 한다.

love, friendship, Jack, London, Seoul, paper, salt, money, water ...

Jack and Emily are studying in the library. Jack과 Emily는 도서관에서 공부하고 있다.

Could you pass me the **salt**, please? 소금 좀 건네주실래요?

I don't have much **money**. 나는 돈이 많지 않다.

There is little **water** in the bottle. 병에 물이 거의 없다.

Practice

Answers p.08

A 다음 괄호 안에 주어진 명사를 적절한 형태로 바꿔 문장을 완성하시오.

1 There are six _____ on the table. (box)

2 The _____ are falling from the tree. (leaf)

3 Becky has seven _____ on her farm. (sheep)

4 I saw two _____ in his apartment last week. (mouse)

5 We have fourteen _____ on our football team. (man)

6 Anne has a large family. She has six _____. (child)

B 다음 〈보기〉에서 알맞은 단어를 골라 단수형이나 복수형으로 바꿔 문장을 완성하시오.

셀 수 있는 명사의 복수형 앞에는 many, few, a few를, 셀 수 없는 명사 앞에는 much, little, a little을 쓴다.

> **보기**   country   story   dog   water   lady   tooth

1 My front _____ is very sore.

2 Vietnam is a _____ in Asia.

3 The _____ are sniffing at the ground.

4 He told me many interesting _____.

5 Edward wanted two bottles of _____.

6 There are two old _____ in the restaurant.

C 다음 밑줄 친 부분을 어법에 맞게 고치시오.

셀 수 없는 명사는 단위나 용기를 이용하여 양을 나타낸다.

a cup of coffee
two cups of coffee

a glass of water
five glasses of water

a piece of cake
three pieces of cake

1 Can I borrow a pair of <u>pant</u>?

2 We should drink a lot of <u>waters</u>.

3 She spends her <u>moneys</u> on clothes.

4 Stanton caught three big <u>fishs</u> this afternoon.

5 May I have three <u>glass</u> of orange juice, please?

sore	painful or aching
sniff	to breathe air in through your nose in order to smell something
pair	an object that is made from two similar parts that are joined together
spend ~ on	to use money to pay for something
clothes	the things that people wear to cover their bodies

Grammar
Lesson 2

★ 관사

① 부정관사 a(n): 셀 수 있는 명사의 단수형 앞에 쓴다.

쓰임	예문
막연한 하나 (= one)	She bought **a pretty skirt** yesterday. 그녀는 어제 예쁜 스커트를 샀다. The man is **an honest person**. 그 남자는 정직한 사람이다.
매 ~, ~마다 (= per, every)	Jim goes to the gym twice **a week**. Jim은 일주일에 두 번 헬스클럽에 간다. I play soccer once **a month**. 나는 한 달에 한 번 축구를 한다.

a+첫 발음이 자음인 단어: a week, a student, a year, a day, a university ...
an+첫 발음이 모음인 단어: an hour, an MP3 player, an apple, an umbrella ...

* 부정관사의 바로 뒤에 오는 단어의 발음이 자음으로 시작하면 a, 모음(a, e, i, o, u)으로 시작하면 an을 쓴다.

② 정관사 the: 셀 수 있는 명사와 셀 수 없는 명사 앞에 모두 쓸 수 있다.

쓰임	예문
이미 언급되었거나 알고 있는 것	A girl is sitting on the bench. **The girl** is reading a book. 한 여자아이가 벤치에 앉아 있다. 그 여자아이는 책 한 권을 읽고 있다. Would you close **the window**, please? 창문 좀 닫아주시겠어요?
세상에 하나밖에 없는 것	I will travel around **the world**. 나는 세계 일주를 할 것이다. **The Moon** goes around **the Earth**. 달은 지구 주위를 돈다.
악기 이름 앞	Sophie can play **the piano** well. Sophie는 피아노를 잘 칠 수 있다. He plays **the drums** every day. 그는 매일 드럼을 친다.

③ 관사를 쓰지 않는 경우

쓰임	예문
학과목, 식사, 운동경기 앞	I played **table tennis** with my brother. 나는 형과 탁구를 쳤다. She had a sandwich for **breakfast**. 그녀는 아침 식사로 샌드위치를 먹었다. My favorite subject is **history**. 내가 좋아하는 과목은 역사이다.
by+교통수단	We went to New York **by train**. 우리는 기차로 뉴욕에 갔다. Brian goes to school **by bus**. Brian은 버스를 타고 학교에 간다.
본래의 목적으로 사용된 건물이나 장소	**go to school** 공부하러 학교에 가다 **go to bed** 잠자러 가다 **go to church** 예배 보러 교회에 가다 **go to college** 대학에 다니다 I **go to church** on Sunday. 나는 일요일에 교회에 간다. She goes to **college** in Chicago. 그녀는 시카고에서 대학에 다닌다.

Practice

Answers p.09

A 다음 빈칸에 a나 an을 쓰고, 필요 없는 경우에는 X표 하시오.

1 Do you have _____ MP3 player?

2 He plays _____ baseball with his friends.

3 We walked for _____ hour in the morning.

4 Mrs. Johnson works eight hours _____ day.

5 I had bacon and an egg for _____ lunch.

6 Jennifer bought _____ lemon and _____ orange.

B 다음 밑줄 친 부분을 어법에 맞게 고쳐 쓰시오.

1 He came here <u>by the subway</u>.

2 We couldn't see <u>a moon</u> yesterday.

3 Susan and Billy had <u>a dinner</u> an hour ago.

4 We <u>go to the school</u> from Monday to Friday.

5 I lost my coat. My mother found <u>an coat</u> under my bed.

> **Hint**
>
> 건물이나 장소가 본래의 목적으로 쓰이지 않는 경우에는 정관사 the를 붙인다.
> Mary's diary was under <u>the</u> bed.
> Mary의 일기장은 침대 밑에 있었다.

C 다음 우리말과 같은 뜻이 되도록 문장을 완성하시오.

1 우리 형은 의사이다.

→ My brother is _____ _____.

2 Chris는 하루에 한 번 나에게 전화를 한다.

→ Chris calls me once _____ _____.

3 지구는 태양 주위를 돈다.

→ _____ _____ goes around _____ _____.

4 Catherine은 피아노를 매우 잘 연주한다.

→ Catherine plays _____ _____ very well.

5 Rebecca는 어젯밤 열한 시에 잠자리에 들었다.

→ Rebecca _____ _____ _____ at eleven last night.

Eng-Eng VOCA

subway	a system of underground trains in a city
moon	the round object that moves around the earth
dinner	the main meal of the day that people eat in the evening
lose	to become unable to find someone or something
coat	a piece of clothing that you wear over your other clothes when you are outside

Grammar
Lesson 3

★ 지시대명사

❶ 지시대명사는 사람이나 사물을 가리키는 대명사이다.

	단수형	복수형
가까이 있는 대상	this	these
멀리 있는 대상	that	those

This is my sister, Mary. 이 사람은 내 여동생 Mary이다.

These are my friends, Lydia and Tracy. 이 사람들은 내 친구 Lydia와 Tracy이다.

That is[That's] an umbrella. 저것은 우산이다.

Those are his watches. 저것들은 그의 시계이다.

❷ this[these], that[those]은 명사 앞에서 명사를 꾸며 주는 지시형용사로도 쓰인다.

This tomato spaghetti is very delicious. 이 토마토 스파게티는 매우 맛있다.

Those books are hers. 저 책들은 그녀의 것이다.

★ 부정대명사 one 정해지지 않은 불특정한 사람이나 사물을 가리키는 말

My cell phone is too old. I want a new one. (one = cell phone)
내 휴대 전화는 너무 오래되었다. 나는 새 것을 원한다.

She has three pens: a black one and two red ones. (one = pen, ones = pens)
그녀는 펜 세 개, 즉 검은 펜 한 개와 빨간 펜 두 개를 가지고 있다.

* 앞에서 언급된 명사와 같은 종류의 불특정한 하나를 나타낼 때, one을 쓴다.
  앞에서 언급한 명사가 복수형이면 ones를 쓴다.

★ all, each, every 수 일치에 주의!

all	'모든, 모두의'라는 의미로, 복수 명사를 수식하고 복수 동사가 온다. All students in that school wear school uniforms. 저 학교의 모든 학생들은 교복을 입는다.
each	'각자, 각각(의)'라는 의미로, 단수 명사를 수식하고 단수 동사가 온다. Each student has his or her own computer. 각각의 학생은 자신의 컴퓨터를 가지고 있다.
every	'모든'이라는 의미로, 단수 명사를 수식하고 단수 동사가 온다. Every country has a national flag. 모든 나라는 국기가 있다.

Practice

Answers p.09

A 다음 괄호 안에서 알맞은 것을 고르시오.

1 Are (that / those) boys your friends?

2 I need a ruler. Do you have (one / it)?

3 I lost my bag. I'm looking for (one / it) now.

4 (That / Those) painting on the wall looks nice.

5 (All / Every) man in the office is wearing a tie.

6 (This / These) shoes are perfect. They fit me very well.

7 Every (student / students) in the class is studying quietly.

> **Hint**
> 지시대명사가 동·식물이나 사물인 경우, it이나 they로 받는다.
> A: Is this <u>your backpack</u>?
> 이것은 너의 배낭이니?
> B: No, <u>it</u>'s hers.
> 아니요, 그것은 그녀의 것이에요.

B 다음 밑줄 친 부분을 어법에 맞게 고쳐 쓰시오.

1 <u>This</u> earings are my favorite.

2 This cup is dirty. Can I have a clean <u>it</u>?

3 Every child usually <u>like</u> candies and cookies.

4 She has a car. She washes <u>one</u> twice a week.

5 Each student at our school <u>have</u> his or her own locker.

6 There are many stars in the sky. <u>That</u> are so beautiful.

> **Hint**
> 앞에 나온 명사와 같은 사물을 나타낼 때에는 it을 쓴다. (복수일 경우 them)
> My cell phone is too old. I don't like <u>it</u>.
> (=my cell phone)
> 내 휴대 전화는 너무 오래되었다. 나는 그것을 좋아하지 않는다.

C 다음 우리말과 같은 뜻이 되도록 문장을 완성하시오.

1 그는 저 카메라를 매우 좋아한다.
   → He likes _____ _____ very much.

2 저것들은 그녀가 좋아하는 잡지책이다.
   → _____ _____ her favorite magazines.

3 이 버스는 만원이다. 다음 버스를 기다리자.
   → This bus is full. Let's wait for the next _____.

4 모든 학생들은 일 년에 네 번 시험을 본다.
   → _____ _____ has a test four times a year.

> **Eng-Eng VOCA**
> | | |
> |---|---|
> | ruler | a long flat straight tool for measuring things or drawing straight lines |
> | perfect | having no mistakes or errors |
> | favorite | a person or thing that you like most |
> | locker | a cabinet for keeping personal items |
> | full | containing as much/many as possible |

★ 비인칭 주어 it　시간, 요일, 날짜, 날씨, 계절, 거리, 명암 등을 나타내는 말

❶ 시간

A: What time is it now? 지금 몇 시예요?

B: It's 6:40. 여섯 시 사십 분이에요.

❷ 요일

A: What day is it today? 오늘은 무슨 요일이에요?

B: It's Thursday. 목요일이에요.

❸ 날짜

A: What date is it today? 오늘은 며칠인가요?

B: It's December 2nd. 12월 2일이에요.

❹ 날씨

A: How's the weather today? 오늘 날씨가 어떤가요?

B: It's windy and cloudy. 바람이 불고 흐려요.

❺ 거리

A: How far is it from here to your school? 여기서 학교까지 얼마나 멀어요?

B: It is about three miles. 약 3마일이에요.

A: How long does it take from your house to the hospital? 당신의 집에서 병원까지 얼마나 걸리나요?

B: It takes half an hour by bus. 버스로 30분 정도 걸려요.

❻ 명암

It's dark outside. 밖이 어둡다.

★ 비인칭 주어 it vs. 인칭대명사 it

종류	쓰임	해석
비인칭 주어 it	시간, 요일, 날짜, 날씨, 계절, 거리, 명암 등을 나타내는 말	해석하지 않음
인칭대명사 it	사물이나 동·식물 등을 대신 가리키는 말	그것

It is my birthday today. 오늘은 내 생일이다.

It gets dark early in the winter. 겨울에는 일찍 어두워진다.

It is a wonderful city. 그곳은 멋진 도시이다.

It is a blue dress. 그것은 파란색 드레스이다.

Practice

Answers p.09

A 다음 밑줄 친 it과 쓰임이 같은 것을 〈보기〉에서 골라 쓰시오.

> **보기**　(a) It's Friday.　　　(b) She'll bring it tomorrow.

1 It's my sister's necklace.　　　　　　　　　　　_____

2 It takes ten minutes by car.　　　　　　　　　_____

3 Is it Christine's cell phone?　　　　　　　　　_____

4 It is very humid in summer.　　　　　　　　　_____

B 다음 질문에 알맞은 대답을 〈보기〉에서 골라 쓰시오.

> **보기**　(a) It was Wednesday.　　(b) It is about three kilometers.
> 　　　　(c) It's six thirty.　　　　(d) It's rainy and cloudy.
> 　　　　(e) It was August 10th.

1 What time is it now?　　　　　　　　　　　_____

2 What day was it yesterday?　　　　　　　　_____

3 What date was it yesterday?　　　　　　　_____

4 How is the weather today?　　　　　　　　_____

5 How far is it from your house to the bank?　_____

> **plus**
> 시간을 묻는 다른 표현으로는 'Do
> you have the time?'이 있다.
> A: Do you have the time?
> 　지금 몇 시입니까?
> B: It's 11 p.m.
> 　오후 열한 시입니다.
> 'Do you have time?'은 '시간이 있
> 나요?'라는 의미이다.

C 다음 우리말과 같은 뜻이 되도록 주어진 단어와 it을 이용하여 문장을 완성하시오.

1 오늘은 너의 생일이야. (birthday)

　→ _____

2 올해 겨울은 추웠다. (this winter)

　→ _____

3 밖은 어두운가요? (outside)

　→ _____

4 여기서 시청까지는 한 시간이 걸린다. (from here to City Hall)

　→ _____

> **Hint**
> It+takes+시간 ~. 시간이 ~만큼
> 걸리다

Eng-Eng VOCA

humid	moist and damp
rainy	having a lot of rain
weather	the temperature and other conditions such as sun, rain, and wind
far	at a great distance in space
outside	not inside a building or room

VOCA
in Grammar

Answers p.10

A 다음 주어진 단어에 맞도록 의미를 바르게 연결하시오.

1 friendship •   a. a school that you go to after high school

2 subject   •   b. the feeling or relationship between friends

3 hero   •   c. a person who steals something from another person

4 thief   •   d. an area of knowledge you study at a school

5 college   •   e. a very brave person that a lot of people admire

B 다음 괄호 안에서 알맞은 것을 고르시오.

1 We need three (car / cars).

2 There is little (water / waters) in the bottle.

3 My grandfather has twelve (deer / deers).

4 The man is (a / an) honest person.

5 They went to New York by (X / the) train.

C 다음 〈보기〉에서 알맞은 단어를 골라 문장을 완성하시오.

> **보기**   one   all   it   each   these

1 _____ is December 2nd.

2 _____ are my friends, Lydia and Tracy.

3 _____ student has his or her own computer.

4 My camera is too old. I want a new _____.

5 _____ students in that school wear school uniforms.

48

Chapter
06
형용사/부사/비교

Lesson 1 형용사
Lesson 2 부사
Lesson 3 비교급/최상급의 형태 ★ 비교급/최상급 구문

Grammar
Lesson 1

★ **형용사** 명사나 대명사를 수식하거나 설명하는 말로, 사람이나 사물의 성질이나 상태를 나타낸다.

❶ 형용사의 역할

▷ 형용사는 명사나 대명사를 앞이나 뒤에서 수식한다.

Kelly bought a **new** computer. Kelly는 새 컴퓨터를 샀다.

They saw an **interesting** movie. 그들은 재미있는 영화를 보았다.

She wants **something cold** to drink. 그녀는 차가운 마실 것을 원한다.

* –thing, –body, –one으로 끝나는 대명사는 반드시 뒤에서 수식한다.

▷ 주어나 목적어를 보충 설명한다.

You look **sad** today. (주격보어) 너는 오늘 슬퍼 보인다.

Edward is **kind** and **handsome**. (주격보어) Edward는 친절하고 잘생겼다.

I found **the book difficult**. (목적격보어) 나는 그 책이 어렵다고 느꼈다.
The news made **us happy**. (목적격보어) 그 소식은 우리를 행복하게 해주었다.

❷ 부정수량형용사 정해져 있지 않은 수나 양을 나타냄

	셀 수 있는 명사(수)	셀 수 없는 명사(양)	수 또는 양(모두)
많은	many	much	a lot of, lots of, plenty of
몇몇의, 약간의	a few	a little	some, any
거의 없는	few	little	—

I met **many**[a lot of, lots of] people at summer camp. 나는 여름 캠프에서 많은 사람들을 만났다.
I don't have **much**[a lot of, lots of] money. 나는 돈이 많지 않다.

Emma eats **a lot of** vegetables. Emma는 채소를 많이 먹는다.
There is **a lot of** food on the table. 탁자 위에 음식이 많이 있다.

Jason has **a few** friends in London. Jason은 런던에 친구가 몇 명 있다.
Richard has **few** pencils in his pencil case. Richard는 필통에 연필이 거의 없다.

❸ some과 any

some	'약간의'라는 뜻으로, 셀 수 있는 명사와	긍정문
any	셀 수 없는 명사 앞에 모두 쓰임	부정문, 의문문

I want to buy **some** orange juice. 나는 오렌지 주스를 좀 사고 싶다.

Bill didn't spend **any** money today. Bill은 오늘 돈을 조금도 쓰지 않았다.

Do you have **any** plans for this summer vacation? 이번 여름 방학에 특별한 계획이 있니?

Practice

Answers p.10

A 다음 괄호 안에서 알맞은 것을 고르시오.

1 He has (a few / a little) classes today.

2 There isn't (much / many) water in the bucket.

3 There were (many / much) people at the store.

4 I had (some / any) soup for breakfast this morning.

5 We don't have (some / any) special plans for our dinner party.

6 David visited (a few / a little) countries during summer vacation.

B 다음 우리말과 같은 뜻이 되도록 〈보기〉에서 알맞은 형용사를 찾아 빈칸에 써 넣으시오.

> 보기   wrong   delicious   beautiful   scary

1 Peter는 무서운 영화를 좋아한다.
→ Peter likes _____ movies.

2 도시 근처에 아름다운 호수가 있다.
→ There is a _____ lake near the city.

3 이 컴퓨터에는 잘못된 것이 아무것도 없다.
→ There is nothing _____ with this computer.

4 엄마는 가족을 위해 맛있는 음식을 요리하신다.
→ My mother cooks _____ food for family.

C 다음 밑줄 친 부분을 어법에 맞게 고쳐 쓰시오.

1 I like <u>comfortably</u> shoes.

2 She told me many <u>thing</u> about you.

3 There is <u>heavy something</u> in the box.

4 There was <u>new nothing</u> in this magazine.

5 He didn't buy <u>some</u> books at the bookstore.

6 We saw <u>a little</u> famous paintings at the museum.

Eng-Eng VOCA

plan	something you have decided to do
delicious	very pleasant to taste
scary	frightening
comfortable	making you feel physically relaxed
museum	a building where interesting and valuable things are shown to people

Grammar
Lesson 2

★ **부사** 문장에서 동사, 형용사, 다른 부사 또는 문장 전체를 수식한다.

She spoke quietly. (동사 수식) 그녀는 조용히 말했다.

The final exams were very easy. (형용사 수식) 기말고사는 매우 쉬웠다.

He walks very fast. (부사 수식) 그는 매우 빨리 걷는다.

Luckily, we found a cheap apartment. (문장 수식) 운이 좋게도 우리는 값이 싼 아파트를 찾았다.

❶ 부사의 형태

대부분의 형용사	형용사 + -ly	quickly, safely, nicely, clearly, kindly, quietly, largely, slowly, carefully ...	
-y로 끝나는 형용사	y → i + -ly	easy → easily lucky → luckily	happy → happily angry → angrily

My father drives carefully. 아버지는 조심스럽게 운전을 하신다.

I closed the door quietly. 나는 조용히 문을 닫았다.

They found the house easily. 그들은 그 집을 쉽게 찾았다.

The girl is smiling happily. 그 소녀는 행복하게 웃고 있다.

❷ 빈도부사 어떤 일이 얼마나 자주 일어나는지를 나타냄

always 항상	usually 대개	often 주로	sometimes 때때로	never 전혀 ~ 않는

She is always kind to us. 그녀는 항상 우리에게 친절하다.

They are usually very careful. 그들은 대개 매우 신중하다.

I often keep an English diary. 나는 종종 영어 일기를 쓴다.

Jacob sometimes writes a postcard to me. Jacob은 가끔 내게 엽서를 쓴다.

We'll never forget your kindness. 우리는 결코 네 친절을 잊지 않을 것이다.

＊ 빈도부사는 be동사나 조동사 뒤, 일반동사 앞에 위치한다.

❸ too와 either

Catherine likes movies. Jason likes movies, too. Catherine은 영화를 좋아한다. Jason도 영화를 좋아한다.

Nick doesn't like milk. Jane doesn't like milk, either. Nick은 우유를 좋아하지 않는다. Jane도 우유를 좋아하지 않는다.

＊ too와 either는 '또한, 역시'라는 뜻으로, too는 긍정문에서, either는 부정문에서 쓰인다.

Practice

Answers p.10

A 다음 괄호 안에서 알맞은 것을 고르시오.

1 My sister always acts (wise / wisely).

2 Jack came into the room (quiet / quietly).

3 This new MP3 player works (good / well).

4 Sophia wasn't (happy / happily) at the news.

5 This is very (important / importantly) information.

> **Plus**
> friendly, lovely는 부사가 아닌 「명사+-ly」형태의 형용사이므로 주의한다.
> Jennifer is a friendly girl.
> Jennifer는 다정한 소녀이다.
> My neighbor George is a very lovely kid.
> 내 이웃 George는 매우 사랑스러운 아이다.

B 다음 밑줄 친 부분을 어법에 맞게 고쳐 쓰시오.

1 You should cross the street <u>careful</u>.

2 Kathy <u>never will stay</u> in South America.

3 We want to walk on the <u>cleanly</u> streets.

4 Her mother is a very <u>beautifully</u> woman.

5 I joined the club. Mike joined the club, <u>either</u>.

6 Brian and I <u>go often</u> to the movies on weekends.

> **Hint**
> 빈도부사는 be동사나 조동사 뒤, 일반동사 앞에 위치한다.

C 다음 우리말과 같은 뜻이 되도록 주어진 단어를 배열하여 문장을 완성하시오.

1 나는 결코 너를 떠나지 않을 것이다. (leave, I, you, will, never)

→ _____

2 John은 아침으로 종종 시리얼을 먹는다. (often, for breakfast, John, cereal, eats)

→ _____

3 어린아이들은 외국어를 매우 쉽게 배운다. (young, very, foreign languages, easily, learn, children)

→ _____

4 Christine은 때때로 엄마를 위해 식료품점에 간다. (for her mother, goes, sometimes, Christine, to the grocery store)

→ _____

> **Eng-Eng VOCA**
>
> | important | having serious meaning or worth; having power or influence |
> |---|---|
> | information | facts or details about someone/something |
> | join | to become a member of a group |
> | foreign | coming from or belonging to a different country |
> | language | the system of communication in speech and writing |

Grammar
Lesson 3

모바일단어장

★ 비교급/최상급의 형태 형용사나 부사의 비교급은 -(e)r이나 more를 붙이고, 최상급은 -(e)st나 most를 붙인다.

대부분의 경우	-er/-est	cheap – cheaper – cheapest hard – harder – hardest	old – older – oldest tall – taller – tallest
-e로 끝나는 경우	-r/-st	nice – nicer – nicest large – larger – largest	wise – wiser – wisest safe – safer – safest
「단모음+단자음」으로 끝나는 경우	자음 한 번 더 쓰고 +-er/-est	fat – fatter – fattest hot – hotter – hottest	big – bigger – biggest thin – thinner – thinnest
-y로 끝나는 경우	y → i +-er/-est	pretty – prettier – prettiest happy – happier – happiest	busy – busier – busiest easy – easier – easiest
대부분의 2음절, 3음절 이상의 단어	more/most +원급	famous – more famous – most famous beautiful – more beautiful – most beautiful interesting – more interesting – most interesting	
불규칙변화		good 좋은/well 건강한, 잘 – better – best bad 나쁜/badly 나쁘게/ill 병이 든 – worse – worst many (수가) 많은/much (양이) 많은 – more – most little (양이) 적은 – less – least	

★ 비교급/최상급 구문

❶ 원급 비교

> as + 형용사/부사의 원급 + as '~만큼 …한'
> not + as[so] + 형용사/부사의 원급 + as '~만큼 …하지 않는(부정)'

Jessica is **as tall as** her brother. Jessica는 그녀의 오빠만큼 키가 크다.

Sally studied **as hard as** Anna (did). Sally는 Anna만큼 열심히 공부했다.

His desk is **not as large as** my desk. 그의 책상은 나의 책상만큼 크지 않다.

Cindy speaks Japanese **as well as** Will (does). Cindy는 Will만큼 일본어를 잘한다.

❷ 비교급: 비교급+than+비교 대상 '~보다 더 …한'

I like spaghetti **better than** pizza. 나는 피자보다 스파게티를 더 좋아한다.

My father is **stronger than** my brother. 아버지는 형보다 힘이 더 세다.

This book is **more interesting** than that one. 이 책은 저 책보다 더 재미있다.

❸ 최상급: the+최상급+(명사) '가장 ~한'

What is **the highest mountain** in the world? 세계에서 가장 높은 산은 무엇입니까?

This is **the best food** in our restaurant. 이것은 우리 식당에서 가장 좋은 음식이다.

Angela is **the tallest girl** of us all. Angela는 우리 모두 중에서 가장 키가 큰 소녀이다.

Practice

A 다음 괄호 안에 주어진 지시대로 빈칸을 채우시오.

1 Edward is _____ _____ in his family. (short, 최상급)

2 This umbrella is _____ _____ that one. (cheap, 비교급)

3 Emily is _____ and _____ _____ her sister. (tall, heavy, 비교급)

4 I can't play the violin _____ _____ _____ Joe. (well, 원급)

5 She is _____ _____ _____ her sister. (not, old, 원급)

B 다음 문장에서 틀린 부분을 찾아 어법에 맞게 고쳐 쓰시오.

1 Firefighters are the most brave.

2 Your house is smaller as his house.

3 Taekwondo is not as easier as yoga.

4 My test score was badder than yours.

5 Johnny Depp's new movie is good than his last one.

비교하는 대상은 문법적으로 같은 요소여야 한다.

My brother's hair is as short as yours.
　(=your hair)
내 동생의 머리 길이는 네 머리 길이만큼 짧다.

My brother's hair is as short as you. (X)

C 다음 우리말과 같은 뜻이 되도록 주어진 단어를 이용하여 문장을 완성하시오.

1 너의 문제는 나의 문제보다 더 심각하다. (serious)
　→ Your problem is _____ _____ _____ mine.

2 그의 자전거는 그녀의 것만큼 오래되지 않았다. (old)
　→ His bicycle is _____ _____ _____ _____ hers.

3 축구는 브라질에서 가장 인기 있는 스포츠이다. (popular)
　→ Soccer is _____ _____ _____ _____ in Brazil.

4 그것은 하늘에서 가장 빛나는 별이다. (bright)
　→ It is _____ _____ _____ in the sky

Eng-Eng VOCA

cheap	lower in price than you expected
heavy	having great weight
brave	dealing courageously with danger
problem	a thing that is difficult to deal with or to understand
popular	liked or enjoyed by many people

VOCA
in Grammar

Answers p.11

A 다음 주어진 단어에 맞도록 의미를 바르게 연결하시오.

1 cheap •   a. to not remember something

2 safe •   b. having good luck

3 lucky •   c. not in danger of being harmed

4 forget •   d. lower in price than you expected

5 kindness •   e. kind behavior towards someone

B 다음 괄호 안에서 알맞은 것을 고르시오.

1 You look (sad /sadly).

2 She spoke (quiet / quietly).

3 The final exams were very (easy / easily).

4 I met (many / much) people at summer camp.

5 Bill wants to buy (some / any) orange juice.

C 다음 〈보기〉에서 알맞은 단어를 골라 문장을 완성하시오.

보기	fluently	stronger	best	tall	better

1 Jessica is as _____ as her brother.

2 Cindy speaks Japanese as _____ as Brian.

3 I like spaghetti _____ than pizza.

4 My father is _____ than my brother.

5 This is the _____ food in our restaurant.

Chapter
07

to부정사와 동명사

Lesson 1   to부정사
Lesson 2   동명사
Lesson 3   to부정사와 동명사 ★ 동사원형을 목적격보어로 취하는 동사 ★ to부정사와 동명사의 관용 표현

Grammar
Lesson 1

★ to부정사

to부정사는 「to+동사원형」의 형태로, 동사의 의미와 성질을 가지면서 문장에서 명사, 형용사, 부사 역할을 한다.

❶ to부정사의 명사적 쓰임 to부정사는 문장에서 주어, 목적어, 보어 역할을 하며, '~하기, ~하는 것'으로 해석한다.

▷ 주어 역할

To ride a motorcycle is dangerous. 오토바이를 타는 것은 위험하다.

To get up early is very difficult. 아침에 일찍 일어나는 것은 매우 힘들다.

To study English is interesting. 영어를 공부하는 것은 재미있다.

▷ 보어 역할

My plan is to collect teddy bears. 나의 계획은 곰 인형을 모으는 것이다.

Her dream is to be a scientist. 그녀의 꿈은 과학자가 되는 것이다.

His goal is to lose five kilograms. 그의 목표는 5kg을 감량하는 것이다.

▷ 목적어 역할

I decided to go camping with my friends. 나는 친구들과 캠핑을 가기로 결정했다.

We hope to see you again. 우리는 너를 다시 보기 바란다.

Jessica wants to live in America. Jessica는 미국에서 살기를 원한다.

❷ to부정사의 형용사적 쓰임 to부정사는 (대)명사를 뒤에서 꾸며주는 형용사 역할을 하며, '~할'이라고 해석한다.

I need something to eat. 나는 먹을 것이 필요하다.

He has many friends to help him. 그는 그를 도와줄 친구들이 많이 있다.

They have a lot of homework to do. 그들은 해야 할 숙제가 많다.

❸ to부정사의 부사적 쓰임 to부정사는 동사, 형용사, 다른 부사 등을 꾸며주는 부사 역할을 하며, 목적, 원인, 결과 등을 나타낸다.

형용사 수식 (~하기에)	**This math problem is difficult to solve.** 이 수학 문제는 풀기 어렵다.
목적 (~하기 위해서)	**I went to London to study English.** 나는 영어를 공부하려고 런던에 갔다.
감정의 원인 (~하게 되어)	**I was happy to pass the exam.** 나는 시험에 통과해서 기뻤다.
결과 (~해서 결국 …하다)	**She grew up to be a nurse.** 그녀는 자라서 간호사가 되었다.

Practice

Answers p.11

A 다음 괄호 안의 주어진 동사를 알맞은 형태로 고쳐 쓰시오.

1 We got up early _____ the train. (take)

2 This is a good place _____ the sunrise. (see)

3 Laura saved some money _____ a bag. (buy)

4 She bought some strawberries _____ jam. (make)

5 Rachel hopes _____ a popular singer. (become)

B 다음 〈보기〉에서 알맞은 동사를 골라 to부정사로 바꿔 문장을 완성하시오.

보기	build	come	read	sleep	wear

1 He was looking for a novel _____.

2 She decided _____ back home.

3 _____ late is bad for your health.

4 They planned _____ a new bridge.

5 My brother found a tie _____.

C 다음 우리말과 같은 뜻이 되도록 문장을 완성하시오.

1 롤러코스터를 타는 것은 매우 신난다.

→ _____ a roller coaster is exciting.

2 나는 대학에서 의학을 공부하기를 원한다.

→ I want _____ medicine in college.

3 Paul은 새 바지를 살 돈이 없다.

→ Paul doesn't have money _____ new pants.

4 Cathy는 외국 친구들을 사귀기 위해 영어를 배운다.

→ Cathy learns English _____ foreign friends.

Eng-Eng VOCA

sunrise	the time when the sun first appears in the morning
save	to keep money instead of spending it
health	the condition of a person's body
bridge	a structure built over something (such as a river) that allows people or vehicles to cross
medicine	the study and treatment of illnesses and injuries

Grammar
Lesson 2

★ 동명사

동명사는 「동사원형＋-ing」의 형태로, 동사의 의미나 성질을 가지면서 문장에서 명사처럼 쓰여 주어, 목적어, 보어 역할을 한다.
이때 동명사는 '~하기', '~하는 것'으로 해석한다.

❶ 주어 역할

Writing an essay is not easy. 에세이를 쓰는 것은 쉽지 않다.

Talking with Eric is very boring. Eric과 이야기하는 것은 매우 지루하다.

Playing basketball with my friends is fun. 친구들과 농구를 하는 것은 재미있다.

❷ 보어 역할

My job is helping poor people. 나의 직업은 가난한 사람들을 도와주는 것이다.

Steven's dream is making a movie. Steven의 꿈은 영화를 만드는 것이다.

His hobby is collecting stamps from different countries. 그의 취미는 여러 나라의 우표를 수집하는 것이다.

❸ 목적어 역할

I love listening to classical music. 나는 고전음악 듣는 것을 좋아한다.

He finished doing his homework. 그는 숙제를 끝마쳤다.

My mother enjoys baking cookies. 어머니는 쿠키 굽는 것을 즐긴다.

❹ 전치사의 목적어 역할

Thank you for inviting us. 우리를 초대해 주셔서 고마워요.

We're afraid of missing the bus. 우리는 버스를 놓칠까 봐 걱정하고 있다. (miss: ~을 놓치다)

Jennifer is good at drawing pictures. Jennifer는 그림을 잘 그린다.

❺ 동명사 vs. 진행형

	형태	의미	쓰임
동명사	동사원형＋-ing	~하기, ~하는 것	명사(주어, 보어, 목적어)
진행형	be동사＋동사원형＋-ing	~하고 있다	동사

My hobby is singing songs. (동명사) 내 취미는 노래 부르는 것이다.

He is singing a song on the stage. (진행형) 그는 무대에서 노래를 부르고 있다.

Ashley loves cooking Mexican food. (동명사) Ashley는 멕시코 음식을 요리하는 것을 좋아한다.

Ashley was cooking dinner for me. (진행형) Ashley는 나를 위해 저녁을 만들고 있었다.

Practice

Answers p.12

A 다음 밑줄 친 동명사의 쓰임과 같은 것을 〈보기〉에서 골라 쓰시오.

> **보기** (a) <u>Seeing</u> is believing.
> (b) Eric's dream is <u>becoming</u> a teacher.
> (c) Anna enjoys <u>meeting</u> new people.
> (d) I'm interested in <u>taking</u> photos.

1 We learned about <u>gardening</u>.　　　　　_____

2 <u>Riding</u> a horse is very exciting.　　　　_____

3 Her goal is <u>having</u> her own car.　　　　_____

4 He didn't mind <u>opening</u> the window.　　_____

> **Plus** 주어나 보어로 쓰인 동명사는 to부정 사로 바꿔 쓸 수도 있다.
> My job is <u>helping</u> poor people.
> = My job is <u>to help</u> poor people.
> 　내 직업은 가난한 사람들을 도와주 는 것이다.

B 다음 〈보기〉에서 알맞은 동사를 골라 동명사로 바꿔 문장을 완성하시오.

> **보기**　join　　spend　　study　　read　　drive

1 _____ fast is very dangerous.

2 We talked about _____ a book club.

3 I enjoy _____ time with my younger sister.

4 My mother loves _____ wild flowers and plants.

5 He finished _____ the newspaper ten minutes ago.

C 다음 밑줄 친 부분이 동명사인지 진행형인지 구분하시오.

1 I am <u>listening</u> to the radio.　　　　　　　_____

　My hobby is <u>listening</u> to the radio.　　　_____

2 <u>Eating</u> fast food is bad for your health.　_____

　Barry is <u>eating</u> a hamburger now.　　　　_____

3 Becky doesn't like <u>going</u> to the hospital.　_____

　Becky is <u>going</u> to the hospital.　　　　　_____

> **Eng-Eng VOCA**
>
> | interested | wanting to learn more about something |
> |---|---|
> | goal | something that you hope to achieve |
> | mind | to dislike something; to worry about someone/something |
> | dangerous | likely to harm someone or to damage something |
> | wild | living in nature, not controlled by people |

Grammar
Lesson 3

★ to부정사와 동명사

❶ to부정사를 목적어로 취하는 동사: hope, want, decide, plan 등

I **want to meet** her soon. 나는 조만간 그녀를 보기를 원한다.

My brother **decided to go** to college. 우리 형은 대학에 가기로 결심했다.

She **planned to exercise** every day. 그녀는 매일 운동하기로 계획을 세웠다.

❷ 동명사를 목적어로 취하는 동사: enjoy, finish, give up, mind 등

We **enjoy playing** badminton after school. 우리는 방과 후에 배드민턴 치는 것을 즐긴다.

I **finished writing** a report. 나는 보고서 쓰는 것을 끝마쳤다.

Would you **mind opening** the door, please? 문을 열어 주시겠어요?

❸ to부정사와 동명사를 목적어로 취하는 동사: begin, start, like, love 등

It **started to snow.** 눈이 내리기 시작했다.

= It **started snowing.**

I **like to play** volleyball. 나는 배구 하는 것을 좋아한다.

= I **like playing** volleyball.

★ 동사원형을 목적격보어로 취하는 동사

▷ 「사역동사(let, have, make)+목적어+동사원형」 ~가 …하도록 시키다

He **let** me **use** his computer. 그는 나에게 컴퓨터를 쓰게 해주었다.

The news **made** me **feel** sad. 그 소식은 나를 슬프게 만들었다.

▷ 「지각동사(see, hear 등)+목적어+동사원형」 ~가 …하는 것을 보다[듣다]

We **heard** Mary **play** the violin. 우리는 Mary가 바이올린을 연주하는 것을 들었다.

★ to부정사와 동명사의 관용 표현

too+형용사+to부정사 너무 ~해서 …할 수 없다	She was **too** busy **to call** him. 그녀는 너무 바빠서 그에게 전화할 수 없었다.
형용사+enough+to부정사 ~할 만큼 충분히 …하다 enough+명사+to부정사 ~할 만큼 충분한 …	She is rich **enough to buy** a sports car. 그녀는 스포츠카를 살 만큼 부유하다. I don't have **enough** money **to buy** a new computer. 나는 새 컴퓨터를 살 만한 충분한 돈이 없다.
go ~ing ~하러 가다	I **went skiing** with my friends last winter. 나는 지난겨울에 친구들과 함께 스키 타러 갔다.
How[What] about ~ing? ~하는 것이 어때?	**How[What] about sitting** down on the bench? 벤치에 앉는 게 어때?

Practice

Answers p.12

A 다음 괄호 안의 동사를 to부정사나 동명사로 바꿔 문장을 완성하시오.

1 I want _____ a lot of money. (make)

2 What about _____ to the beach this afternoon? (go)

3 My father gave up _____ cigarettes. (smoke)

4 Did your brother finish _____ his sneakers? (wash)

5 Edward planned _____ a party at his house. (have)

6 He will go _____ with his daughter tomorrow. (hike)

B 다음 밑줄 친 부분을 바르게 고쳐 쓰시오.

1 How about <u>to eat</u> pizza for lunch?

2 I don't mind <u>to drive</u> if you're tired.

3 I was too tired <u>to going</u> to the movies last night.

4 Mr. White made his daughter <u>to study</u> abroad.

5 We have enough time <u>finishing</u> our final report.

C 다음 우리말과 같은 뜻이 되도록 문장을 완성하시오.

plus
「How[What] about –ing」는
「Let's+동사원형」과 바꿔쓸 수 있다.
<u>How[What] about going</u> to
the beach?
= <u>Let's go</u> to the beach.
해변에 가자.

1 그녀에게 엽서를 쓰는 게 어때?
   → How about _____ a postcard to her?

2 Ashley는 지난여름에 가족과 함께 서핑하러 갔다.
   → Ashley _____ _____ with her family last summer.

3 그들은 파리에 있는 조부모님을 방문하려고 계획했다.
   → They planned _____ _____ their grandparents in Paris.

4 Steve는 이 상자들을 나를 만큼 충분히 힘이 세다.
   → Steve is strong enough _____ _____ these boxes.

Eng-Eng VOCA	
give up	to stop doing something, especially something that you do regularly
hike	to take a long walk in the mountains or countryside
abroad	in or to a foreign country
final	happening or coming at the end
carry	to take someone/something from one place to another

VOCA
in Grammar

Answers p.12

A 다음 주어진 단어에 맞도록 의미를 바르게 연결하시오.

1 collect • a. to stop doing something

2 lose • b. to get things of the same type from different places

3 bake • c. to fail to keep or to maintain

4 mind • d. to feel upset about something

5 give up • e. to cook food in an oven

B 다음 괄호 안에서 알맞은 것을 고르시오.

1 I (like / want) playing volleyball.

2 I (finished / hoped) writing a report.

3 Edward (let / mind) me use his computer.

4 She (enjoyed / planned) to exercise every day.

5 My brother (decided / gave up) to go to college.

C 다음 〈보기〉에서 알맞은 단어를 골라 문장을 완성하시오.

> **보기**　　baking　　inviting　　made　　play　　going

1 The news _____ me feel sad.

2 Thank you for _____ us.

3 My mother enjoys _____ cookies.

4 We heard Mary _____ the violin.

5 How about _____ to the beach?

Chapter
08
문장의 형태

Lesson 1 문장의 구성요소   1형식   2형식
Lesson 2 3형식   4형식   5형식

Grammar
Lesson 1

★ 문장의 구성요소

❶ 주어(Subject): 동작을 행하는 주체로, '~은, 는, 이, 가'로 해석한다.

> You are handsome. 너는 잘생겼다.
>
> Britney likes flowers. Britney는 꽃을 좋아한다.

❷ 동사(Verb): 주어의 동작이나 상태를 나타내는 말로, '~(이)다, ~하다'로 해석한다.

> I wrote a letter to you. 나는 너에게 편지를 썼다.
>
> The book is on the table. 그 책은 테이블 위에 있다.

❸ 보어(Complement): 주어나 목적어의 성질이나 상태 등을 보충해 주는 말로, 주격보어와 목적격보어가 있다.

> My uncle is a doctor. 우리 삼촌은 의사다.
>
> She makes me happy. 그녀는 나를 행복하게 해 준다.

❸ 목적어(Object): 동사가 나타내는 동작의 대상이 되는 말로, '~을, 를'로 해석한다.

> I can speak Chinese. 나는 중국어를 할 줄 안다.
>
> My mother bought a car. 우리 엄마는 자동차를 사셨다.

★ 1형식 주어(S)+동사(V)

> The phone rang. 전화벨이 울렸다.
>
> Tom dances well. Tom은 춤을 잘 춘다.
>
> The baby is crying in the room. 아기가 방에서 울고 있다.
>
> A dog is behind you. 개 한 마리가 네 뒤에 있다.

★ 2형식 주어(S)+동사(V)+보어(C)

❶ 주격보어는 주어를 보충 설명한다.

> You seem happy. 너는 행복해 보인다. (seem: ~처럼 보이다)
>
> He became a good violinist. 그는 훌륭한 바이올리니스트가 되었다.
>
> My puppy is cute. 내 강아지는 귀엽다.

❷ 감각동사(look, sound, smell, taste, feel ...)+형용사

> John looks busy. John은 바빠 보인다.
>
> It smells great. 그것은 좋은 냄새가 난다.
>
> This coffee tastes fresh. 이 커피는 신선한 맛이 난다.
>
> I felt happy to hear the news. 나는 그 소식을 들어서 행복했다.

Practice

Answers p.13

A 다음 〈보기〉와 같이 문장 구성요소에 밑줄 긋고, S(주어), V(동사), C(보어)로 표시하시오.

> **보기**
> Jane became a teacher.
> S   V   C

1 My brother sang.

2 Miranda and Jack ran.

3 The stew smells bad.

4 This machine looks strange.

5 Teddy is a very diligent student.

B 다음 괄호 안에서 알맞은 것을 고르시오.

> **Hint**
> 감각동사 뒤에 부사를 쓰지 않도록 주의한다.
> (O) He looks nice. (형용사)
>   그는 좋아 보인다.
> (X) He looks nicely. (부사)

1 It sounds (great / greatly).

2 I felt very (hungry / hungrily).

3 The spaghetti tastes (good / well).

4 The bread smells (terrible / terribly).

5 Jennifer looks (beautiful / beautifully).

C 다음 우리말과 같은 뜻이 되도록 주어진 단어를 배열하여 문장을 완성하시오.

1 나는 매우 목마름을 느꼈다. (thirsty, felt, I, very)

→ _____

2 그의 이름은 Daniel이다. (his, is, name, Daniel)

→ _____

3 그 수프는 맛있는 냄새가 난다. (smells, delicious, the soup)

→ _____

4 그녀는 유명한 의사가 되었다. (famous, became, doctor, she, a)

→ _____

Eng-Eng VOCA

machine	a piece of equipment that does a particular job by using power (such as electricity)
strange	different from what is usual, normal, or expected
taste	to have a particular flavor
terrible	very bad, shocking or unpleasant
thirsty	needing or wanting to drink

Grammar
Lesson 2

★ 3형식 주어(S)+동사(V)+목적어(O)

I made cookies for you. 나는 너를 위해 쿠키를 만들었다.

She likes classical music. 그녀는 고전 음악을 좋아한다.

★ 4형식 주어(S)+수여동사(V)+간접목적어(IO)+직접목적어(DO)

❶ 수여동사: '~에게(간접목적어)'와 '~을[를](직접목적어)'의 의미를 갖는 두 개의 목적어를 취한다.

I sent my grandparents a letter. 나는 조부모님께 편지를 보냈다.
S V   IO   DO

Leo gave me a present. Leo가 나에게 선물을 주었다.
S   V   IO   DO

❷ 문장의 전환(4형식 → 3형식): 간접목적어와 직접목적어의 순서를 바꾸고 간접목적어 앞에 전치사 to, for, of를 쓴다.

▷ to를 취하는 동사: give, send, show, teach, bring, lend, write, tell, pass ...

She showed me her paintings. (4형식) 그녀는 내게 그녀의 그림들을 보여주었다.
         IO   DO

→ She showed her paintings to me. (3형식)
            DO   IO

▷ for를 취하는 동사: make, buy, cook, get ...

My father bought my mother a ring. (4형식) 아버지는 어머니에게 반지를 사주셨다.

→ My father bought a ring for my mother. (3형식)

▷ of를 취하는 동사: ask ...

The policeman asked me some questions. (4형식) 경찰관이 내게 몇 가지 질문을 했다.
→ The policeman asked some questions of me. (3형식)

★ 5형식 주어(S)+동사(V)+목적어(O)+목적격보어(OC)

❶ 목적격보어는 목적어의 성질이나 상태를 보충 설명해 주는 말이다.

My parents call me "Pooh." (me=Pooh) 부모님은 나를 '푸우'라고 부른다.

I found the test difficult. (the test의 상태=difficult) 나는 시험이 어렵다고 느꼈다.

❷ 동사원형을 목적격보어로 취하는 동사

▷ 사역동사(have, let, make)+목적어+동사원형 ~가 ...하도록 시키다

My parents had me study every evening. 부모님은 나에게 매일 저녁 공부하도록 시키신다.

▷ 지각동사(see, hear, feel ...)+목적어+동사원형 ~가 ...하는 것을 보다[듣다, 느끼다]

I saw my mother cook in the kitchen. 나는 우리 어머니가 부엌에서 요리하는 것을 보았다.

I heard someone cry. 나는 누군가 우는 소리를 들었다.

68

Practice

Answers p.13

A 다음 〈보기〉와 같이 문장 구성요소에 밑줄 긋고 S(주어), V(동사), IO(간접목적어), DO(직접목적어), O(목적어), OC(목적격보어)로 표시하시오.

> **Plus**
> 준사역동사 help는 목적격보어로 동사원형과 to부정사를 둘 다 쓸 수 있다.
> I helped her (to) carry her suitcase.
> 나는 그녀가 여행가방을 옮기는 것을 도와주었다.

> **보기**
> He gave me a present.
> S   V   IO   DO
>
> She made me join the club.
> S   V   O   OC

1 I bought my friend a cake.

2 My father told us the story.

3 I saw a baby cry.

4 Jacob makes me laugh.

B 다음 두 문장이 같은 뜻이 되도록 문장을 완성하시오.

1 The reporters asked her many questions.

→ The reporters asked _____ _____ _____ _____.

2 Edward sent me flowers for my birthday.

→ Edward sent _____ _____ _____ for my birthday.

3 My friend made me a pencil case.

→ My friend made _____ _____ _____ _____.

C 다음 우리말과 같은 뜻이 되도록 주어진 단어를 배열하여 문장을 완성하시오.

1 나는 오늘 아침에 그녀에게 그 가방을 가져다주었다. (her, brought, the bag, I)

→ _____ this morning.

2 Liz는 토요일마다 나에게 영어를 가르쳐 준다. (teaches, me, Liz, English)

→ _____ every Saturday.

3 나는 내 친구들이 축구하는 것을 보았다. (my friends, play, I, saw)

→ _____ soccer.

4 그녀는 선생님께 자신의 보고서를 보여드렸다. (showed, to, her, report, she)

→ _____ the teacher.

> **Eng-Eng VOCA**
>
> laugh — to make sounds with your voice to show that you are happy or that something is funny
> reporter — a person who collects and reports news for newspapers, radio or television
> send — to arrange for something to go to another place, especially by post
> birthday — the day when someone was born or the anniversary of that day
> teach — to give someone lessons to help them to learn about a subject

VOCA
in Grammar

Answers p.13

A 다음 주어진 단어에 맞도록 의미를 바르게 연결하시오.

1 seem   •   a. to be aware of sounds with your ears

2 hear   •   b. recently made, produced

3 taste   •   c. to hold something in your hand

4 carry   •   d. to eat or drink a small amount

5 fresh   •   e. to appear to be true

B 다음 괄호 안에서 알맞은 것을 고르시오.

1 The phone (rang / seemed).

2 She (showed / liked) me her painting.

3 His mother (made / taught) him study English.

4 My father bought a ring (for / of) my mother.

5 The policeman asked some questions (for / of) me.

C 다음 〈보기〉에서 알맞은 단어를 골라 문장을 완성하시오.

> 보기   saw   sent   dances   tastes   likes

1 Tom _____ well.

2 The coffee _____ fresh.

3 She _____ classical music.

4 He _____ his grandparents a letter.

5 I _____ my mother cook in the kitchen.

Chapter

09

문장의 종류

Lesson 1 명령문   제안문
Lesson 2 감탄문
Lesson 3 부가의문문
Lesson 4 의문사가 있는 의문문

Grammar
Lesson 1

★ 명령문 상대방에게 어떤 행동을 하거나 하지 말라고 요구하는 문장

❶ 긍정명령문 (∼해라): 동사원형 ∼

Be quiet in the library. 도서관에서는 조용히 해라.

Go straight and turn right. 곧장 가서 오른쪽으로 돌아라.

Close the window, please. (= Please close the window.) 창문 좀 닫아주세요.

❷ 부정명령문 (∼하지 마라): Don't+동사원형 ∼

Don't tell anyone about this. 이것에 대해 누구에게도 말하지 마라.

Don't speak loudly in the classroom. 교실에서는 큰소리로 말하지 마라.

Don't play baseball in the garden. 정원에서 야구하지 마라.

❸ 명령문+and/or

명령문, and ∼ …해라, 그러면 ∼할 것이다	**Study hard, and** you'll pass the exam. 열심히 공부해라, 그러면 너는 시험에 통과할 것이다. **Hurry up, and** you'll be there in time. 서둘러라, 그러면 너는 제 시간에 그곳에 도착할 것이다.
명령문, or ∼ …해라, 그렇지 않으면 ∼할 것이다	**Study hard, or** you'll fail the exam. 열심히 공부해라, 그렇지 않으면 너는 시험에 떨어질 것이다. **Hurry up, or** you'll be late. 서둘러라, 그렇지 않으면 너는 늦을 것이다.

★ 제안문 상대방에게 어떤 행동을 하거나 하지 말자고 권유하거나 제안하는 문장

❶ 긍정제안문

Let's+동사원형 ∼하자	**Let's eat out for dinner.** 저녁은 나가서 먹자.
Shall we+동사원형 ∼? ∼할까요?	**Shall we have a cup of coffee?** 우리 커피 한 잔 할까요?
Why don't we+동사원형 ∼? ∼하는 게 어때?	**Why don't we play computer games tonight?** 오늘 밤에 컴퓨터 게임하는 게 어때?
How about+-ing ∼? ∼하는 게 어때?	**How about going skiing next week?** 다음 주에 스키를 타러 가는 게 어때?

❷ 부정제안문

Let's not+동사원형 ∼하지 말자	**Let's not eat fast food for dinner.** 저녁으로 패스트푸드는 먹지 말자. **Let's not play soccer today.** 오늘은 축구를 하지 말자.

Practice

Answers p.14

A 다음 괄호 안에서 알맞은 것을 고르시오.

1 Kate, (do / does) your best.

2 (Not / Don't) eat during the meeting.

3 (Am / Be) kind and nice to your brother.

4 Hurry up, (and / or) you will catch the train.

5 Wear your coat, (and / or) you'll catch a cold.

6 Why don't we (have / having) lunch at the cafeteria?

B 다음 문장을 괄호 안의 지시대로 바꿔 쓰시오.

1 You should be quiet here. (긍정명령문)

→ _____

2 Let's go for a walk for a while. (shall we 제안문)

→ _____

3 How about going to the museum? (why don't we 제안문)

→ _____

4 You must not cross the street at the red light. (부정명령문)

→ _____

C 다음 우리말과 같은 뜻이 되도록 주어진 단어를 배열하여 문장을 완성하시오.

1 도서관 앞에서 만나자. (in front of, let's, the library, meet)

→ _____

2 서둘러라. 그렇지 않으면 너는 기차를 놓칠 것이다. (miss, will, you, hurry up, or, the train)

→ _____

3 다시는 똑같은 실수를 하지 마라. (don't, again, the same mistake, make)

→ _____

4 이번 일요일에 해변에 가는 게 어때? (to the beach, this Sunday, how, going, about)

→ _____

catch	to be in time for a bus, train, or plane and get on it
cafeteria	a restaurant where you get food at a counter and carry it to a table for eating
for a while	for a short time
cross	to go from one side to the other
miss	to fail to hit, reach, or get something

Grammar
Lesson 2

★ 감탄문 기쁨, 놀람, 슬픔 등의 감정을 표현하는 문장으로, '~하는구나!'라고 해석

❶ What 감탄문: What(+a[an])+형용사+명사(+주어+동사)!

명사 강조	셀 수 있는 단수명사인 경우	Jane is a very smart girl. Jane은 매우 영리한 소녀다. What a smart girl (Jane is)! Jane은 참 영리한 소녀구나!
	셀 수 없는 명사나 복수명사인 경우	Those are very expensive shoes. 저것은 매우 비싼 신발이다. What expensive shoes (those are)! 저것은 참 비싼 신발이구나!

* 셀 수 있는 단수 명사인 경우 형용사 앞에 반드시 a[an]를 붙이고, 복수 명사나 셀 수 없는 명사인 경우 a[an]를 붙이지 않는다.

It is a very delicious Korean dish. 그것은 매우 맛있는 한국 요리다.
→ **What a delicious Korean dish (it is)!** 그것은 참 맛있는 한국 요리구나!

You are a very beautiful girl. 너는 매우 아름다운 소녀다.
→ **What a beautiful girl (you are)!** 너는 참 아름다운 소녀구나!

David has really great ideas. David는 정말 좋은 생각을 가지고 있다.
→ **What great ideas David has!** David는 정말 좋은 생각을 가지고 있구나!

❷ How 감탄문: How+형용사/부사(+주어+동사)!

형용사 강조	You are very beautiful. 너는 매우 예쁘다. How beautiful (you are)! 너는 정말 예쁘구나!
부사 강조	She walks really fast. 그녀는 정말 빨리 걷는다. How fast she walks! 그녀는 참 빨리 걷는구나!

It is really hot. 몹시 덥다.
→ **How hot (it is)!** (형용사 강조) 정말 덥구나!

You are very tall. 너는 키가 매우 크다.
→ **How tall (you are)!** (형용사 강조) 너는 참 키가 크구나!

She studies very hard. 그녀는 매우 열심히 공부한다.
→ **How hard she studies!** (부사 강조) 그녀는 참 열심히 공부하는구나!

Practice

Answers p.14

A 다음 밑줄 친 부분을 어법에 맞게 고쳐 쓰시오.

1 How cute <u>is the puppy</u>!

2 <u>How</u> a lucky boy he is!

3 What <u>a teacher excellent</u> he is!

4 What <u>difficult question</u> that is!

B 다음 문장을 주어진 단어로 시작하는 감탄문으로 바꾸시오.

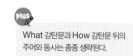

Plus

What 감탄문과 How 감탄문 뒤의
주어와 동사는 종종 생략된다.

1 The movie was so boring.

→ How _____!

2 She is an intelligent girl.

→ What _____!

3 The cell phone is very small.

→ How _____!

4 They are really fantastic dancers.

→ What _____!

5 It was a really wonderful story.

→ What _____!

C 다음 우리말과 같은 뜻이 되도록 주어진 단어를 배열하여 문장을 완성하시오.

1 너는 참 영리하구나! (you, are, how, clever)

→ _____

2 그 오페라는 정말 훌륭했어! (was, great, the opera, how)

→ _____

3 Jenna는 참 부지런한 학생이구나! (Jenna, a, what, diligent, is, student)

→ _____

4 너는 참 멋진 드레스를 입었구나! (dress, a, you, lovely, what, wore)

→ _____

Eng-Eng
VOCA

lucky	having good luck
boring	dull and uninteresting
intelligent	having the ability to easily learn things or to deal with difficult problems
opera	a musical play where actors sing all of the words
diligent	showing care and effort in your work or duties

Grammar
Lesson 3

★ 부가의문문 상대방에게 어떤 사실을 확인하거나 동의를 구할 때 쓴다.

부가의문문은 '그렇지?' 또는 '그렇지 않니'라는 의미로, 문장 뒤에 「동사＋주어」를 덧붙인다.
긍정문에서는 부정으로, 부정문에서는 긍정으로 묻고, 주어는 대명사로 받는다.

❶ be동사의 부가의문문

긍정문의 부가의문문	「주어＋be동사 ~, be동사＋not＋주어(대명사)?」
	Emma is your sister, isn't she? Emma는 네 여동생이지, 그렇지 않니?
	They were very angry, weren't they? 그들은 화가 났었어, 그렇지 않니?
부정문의 부가의문문	「주어＋be동사＋not ~, be동사＋주어(대명사)?」
	This movie isn't interesting, is it? 이 영화는 재미있지 않아, 그렇지?
	You weren't at the party, were you? 너는 파티에 없었지, 그렇지?

❷ 조동사의 부가의문문

긍정문의 부가의문문	「주어＋조동사 ~, 조동사＋not＋주어(대명사)?」
	Mr. Bolton will stay at the hotel, won't he? Bolton 씨는 호텔에 묵을 거야, 그렇지 않니?
	We can pass the exam, can't we? 우리는 시험에 합격할 수 있을 거야, 그렇지 않니?
부정문의 부가의문문	「주어＋조동사＋not ~, 조동사＋주어(대명사)?」
	You can't speak Japanese, can you? 너는 일본어를 할 수 없지, 그렇지?
	Edward won't be late, will he? Edward는 늦지 않을 거야, 그렇지?

❸ 일반동사의 부가의문문

긍정문의 부가의문문	「주어＋일반동사 ~, don't/doesn't/didn't＋주어(대명사)?」
	Your father reads a newspaper, doesn't he? 네 아버지는 신문을 읽으셔, 그렇지 않니?
	You finished your report yesterday, didn't you? 너는 어제 보고서를 끝냈지, 그렇지 않니?
부정문의 부가의문문	「주어＋don't/doesn't/didn't ~, do/does/did＋주어(대명사)?」
	Mrs. Brown doesn't have a car, does she? Brown 부인은 차가 없어, 그렇지?
	Bob and Grace didn't go home, did they? Bob과 Grace는 집에 가지 않았어, 그렇지?

Practice

Answers p.15

A 다음 빈칸에 알맞은 말을 넣어 부가의문문을 완성하시오.

1 It is cold in here, _____ it?

2 Brad will be here soon, won't _____ ?

3 My mother locked the door, _____ she?

4 These stories were very boring, weren't _____ ?

5 Let's have dinner at the restaurant, shall _____ ?

Hint
제안문의 부가의문문은 조동사 shall 을 사용한다.

Let's order pizza, shall we?
피자를 주문하자, 응?

Let's not eat at night, shall we?
밤에는 먹지말자, 응?

B 다음 밑줄 친 부분을 어법에 맞게 고쳐 쓰시오.

1 Jack has an umbrella, <u>don't he</u>?

2 The concert was great, <u>didn't it</u>?

3 Don't park your car here, <u>shall we</u>?

4 We can swim there in the morning, <u>can we</u>?

5 You ordered a cheese spaghetti, <u>weren't you</u>?

Hint
명령문의 부가의문문은 조동사 will을 사용한다.

Come home early, will you?
일찍 집에 와, 그럴 거지?

Don't act like a child, will you?
아이처럼 행동하지 마, 응?

C 다음 우리말과 같은 뜻이 되도록 문장을 완성하시오.

1 Diana는 소개팅을 했어, 그렇지 않니?

→ Diana had a blind date, _____ _____ ?

2 수업 중에는 이야기하지 마라, 그럴 거지?

→ Don't talk during the class, _____ _____ ?

3 네 여동생은 첼로를 연주할 수 없지, 그렇지 않니?

→ Your sister can't play the cello, _____ _____ ?

4 Thomas는 숙제를 안 했어, 그렇지?

→ Thomas didn't do his homework, _____ _____ ?

5 내일 추울 거야, 그렇지 않니?

→ It will be cold tomorrow, _____ _____ ?

Eng-Eng VOCA

lock	to fasten something, usually with a key
park	to put a car or other vehicle in a particular place for a period of time
order	to request food or drinks from a restaurant
blind date	a meeting between two people who have not met each other before
during	from the beginning to the end of a period of time

Grammar
Lesson 4

★ **의문사가 있는 의문문** 의문문의 어순 : 의문사+동사(be동사/조동사/do(es)/did)+주어 ~?

❶ who (누구): 신분이나 관계, 이름 등을 물을 때 쓴다.

A: **Who is the girl on the bench?** 벤치에 앉아 있는 저 소녀는 누구예요?
B: She is <u>my cousin, Sue.</u> 그녀는 내 사촌 Sue예요.

❷ what (무엇): 사물의 이름이나 사람의 직업을 물을 때 쓴다.

A: **What did you eat for lunch?** 점심으로 무엇을 먹었나요?
B: I ate <u>Chinese food</u> for lunch. 저는 중국 음식을 먹었어요.

❸ which (어느 것): 정해진 대상 중에서 선택하는 경우에 쓴다.

A: **Which do you like better, coffee or tea?** 커피와 차 중 어떤 것이 더 좋나요?
B: I like <u>coffee</u> better. 저는 커피를 더 좋아해요..

❹ when (언제): 시간이나 날짜 등을 물을 때 쓴다.

A: **When is your birthday?** 당신의 생일은 언제예요?
B: It was <u>yesterday.</u> 어제였어요.

❺ where (어디에, 어디서): 장소를 물을 때 쓴다.

A: **Where are you from?** 당신은 어디에서 왔나요?
B: I'm from <u>Canada.</u> 저는 캐나다에서 왔어요.

❻ why (왜): 이유를 물을 때 쓴다. 대답은 주로 because(왜냐하면)를 쓴다.

A: **Why did he go to New York?** 그는 왜 뉴욕에 갔나요?
B: He went there <u>because he wanted to study English.</u> 그는 영어를 공부하고 싶어서 뉴욕에 갔어요.

❼ how (어떻게): 수단, 방법, 상태 등을 물을 때 쓴다.

A: **How do you go home?** (수단, 방법) 당신은 어떻게 집에 가나요?
B: I go home <u>by subway.</u> 저는 지하철을 타고 집에 가요.

A: **How is the weather in Seoul?** (상태) 서울의 날씨는 어때요?
B: It's <u>sunny and hot.</u> 화창하고 더워요.

▷ 「How + 형용사/부사」 얼마나 ~한

How old is she? 그녀는 몇 살인가요?
How long is this tunnel? 이 터널은 얼마나 깁니까?
How often do you go shopping? 당신은 얼마나 자주 쇼핑하러 가나요?
How many books do you have? 당신은 얼마나 많은 책을 가지고 있나요?
How much money do you have? 당신은 얼마나 많은 돈을 가지고 있나요?

Practice

Answers p.15

A 다음 질문에 알맞은 대답을 찾아 연결하시오.

의문사가 있는 의문문은 특정한 정보를 묻는 의문문으로, yes나 no로 대답할 수 없다.

1 Where is my smartphone? •   a. She is my sister.

2 When will Jessica leave? •   b. It's on the table.

3 What does your father do? •   c. She will leave at five.

4 Who is the girl with a long hair? •   d. I have two.

5 How many brothers do you have? •   e. He works at a hospital.

B 다음 〈보기〉에서 알맞은 의문사를 골라 대화를 완성하시오.

> **보기**   where   how   why   which

1 A: _____ do you come to school?

   B: I come to school by bus.

2 A: _____ did you go yesterday?

   B: I went to the stadium with Jim.

3 A: _____ didn't she go to the party?

   B: Because she was very busy.

4 A: _____ do you like better, cats or dogs?

   B: I like dogs better.

C 다음 우리말과 같은 뜻이 되도록 주어진 단어를 배열하여 문장을 완성하시오.

의문사가 있는 의문문은 특정한 정보를 묻는 의문문으로, yes나 no로 대답할 수 없다.
How old ~? 나이
How long ~? 길이나 기간
How often ~? 빈도
How many+복수 명사 ~? 수
How much+단수 명사 ~? 양
How far ~? 거리

1 그녀의 가방은 무슨 색입니까? (her, color, what, is, bag)

   → _____

2 저기에 있는 남자는 누구니? (over there, who, the man, is)

   → _____

3 너는 얼마나 자주 축구를 하니? (you, how often, do, play soccer)

   → _____

4 너는 주말에 언제 일어나니? (on weekends, when, get up, do, you)

   → _____

leave	to go away from a place or a person
stadium	a large sports ground surrounded by rows of seats
soccer	a game where two teams try to kick the ball into the other team's goal
get up	to get out of your bed after sleeping
weekend	Saturday and Sunday

VOCA
in Grammar

Answers p.15

A 다음 주어진 단어에 맞도록 의미를 바르게 연결하시오.

1 straight •   a. to do something more quickly than usual

2 fail •   b. an underground, electric railroad in a city

3 loudly •   c. in a direct way

4 hurry •   d. to not succeed in achieving something

5 subway •   e. in a way that makes a lot of noise

B 다음 괄호 안에서 알맞은 것을 고르시오.

1 (Be / Go) quiet in the library.

2 Don't (be / play) baseball in the garden.

3 Let's (eat / eating) pasta for dinner.

4 (What / How) a delicious Korean dish it is!

5 (What / How) hard she studies!

C 다음 〈보기〉에서 알맞은 단어를 골라 문장을 완성하시오.

보기   is   isn't   can   won't   doesn't

1 Your father reads a newspaper, _____ he?

2 You can't speak French, _____ you?

3 Emma is your sister _____ she?

4 This movie isn't interesting, _____ it?

5 Mr. Bolton will stay at the hotel, _____ he?

Chapter 10

접속사와 전치사

Lesson 1 등위접속사
Lesson 2 종속접속사
Lesson 3 시간을 나타내는 전치사
Lesson 4 장소를 나타내는 전치사

Grammar
Lesson 1

★ 등위접속사 문법적으로 대등한 역할을 하는 단어, 구, 절 등을 연결하는 말

❶ and (~와, 그래서, 그리고)

Fred and I play soccer after school. (단어와 단어) Fred와 나는 방과 후에 축구를 한다.

We played games and sang songs. (구와 구) 우리는 게임을 하고 노래를 불렀다.

I listened to the radio, and my father read a book. (절과 절) 나는 라디오를 듣고, 아버지는 책을 읽으셨다.

❷ or (또는, 혹은)

Joe will visit Paris in June or July. (단어와 단어) Joe는 6월이나 7월에 파리를 방문할 예정이다.

You can pay by credit card or in cash. (구와 구) 너는 신용카드나 현금으로 계산할 수 있다.

Did you go to the movies or were you at home last night? (절과 절) 너는 어젯밤에 영화를 보러 갔니, 아니면 집에 있었니?

❸ but (그러나, 그런데)

He is lazy but smart. (단어와 단어) 그는 게으르지만, 영리하다.

The food was a little salty but very tasty. (구와 구) 음식은 약간 짜지만, 매우 맛있었다.

I have a sister, but I don't have a brother. (절과 절) 나는 여동생이 있지만, 남동생은 없다.

❹ so (그래서, 그 결과)

Ann is very kind, so everyone likes her. Ann은 매우 친절해서 모두 그녀를 좋아한다.
　　　원인　　　　　　　　　결과

My room was very cold, so I closed the window. 방이 매우 추워서 나는 창문을 닫았다.
　　　　원인　　　　　　　　　결과

Jack lost his glasses, so he couldn't see anything. Jack은 안경을 잃어버려서 아무것도 볼 수가 없었다.
　　　　원인　　　　　　　　결과

* 등위접속사 so는 and, or, but과는 달리 절과 절을 연결하는 데만 쓰인다.

❺ 셋 이상의 단어, 구, 절을 나열할 때는 쉼표(,)로 연결하고 마지막 것 앞에만 접속사를 쓴다.

He is tall, handsome, and kind. (셋 이상의 단어) 그는 키가 크고, 잘생겼고, 친절하다.

You can go to the airport by bus, by subway, or on foot. (셋 이상의 구)
너는 공항에 버스로, 지하철로, 아니면 걸어서 갈 수 있다.

Practice

Answers p.16

A 다음 괄호 안에서 알맞은 것을 고르시오.

1 Which do you want, green tea (and / or) coffee?

2 They needed some help, (but / so) I helped them.

3 He can speak Chinese, (and / but) he can't write it.

4 I wanted to give him a hint, (but / or) he didn't want one.

5 My mother may be in the kitchen (but / or) in the garden.

6 James borrowed some books (and / but) DVDs at the library.

B 다음 우리말과 같은 뜻이 되도록 문장을 완성하시오.

1 선생님은 매우 친절하지만 엄격하다.

→ My teacher is very kind _____ strict.

2 Cathy는 금발 머리에 파란 눈을 가지고 있다.

→ Cathy has blond hair _____ blue eyes.

3 너는 외출하고 싶니, 아니면 집에 있고 싶니?

› Do you want to go out _____ stay at home?

4 나는 어제 길에서 Emma와 John을 만났다.

→ I met Emma _____ John on the street yesterday.

5 그녀는 우유를 많이 마시지만, 커피는 마시지 않는다.

→ She drinks a lot of milk, _____ she doesn't drink coffee.

C 다음 내용이 자연스럽게 이어지도록 접속사에 유의하여 문장을 연결하시오.

1 Chris missed the bus,   •   a. yellow or green?

2 She didn't have any money, •   b. so he took a taxi.

3 I was very tired,   •   c. but I'll try it again.

4 Which color do you want, •   d. and I went to bed early.

5 I failed the test,   •   e. so she couldn't buy the shoes.

Eng-Eng VOCA

hint	a piece of information that helps you guess an answer or do something
strict	demanding that people follow rules or behave in a certain way
blond	having pale or yellow hair
tired	feeling a need to rest or sleep
fail	to end without success

Grammar
Lesson 2

★ 종속접속사

❶ 종속접속사

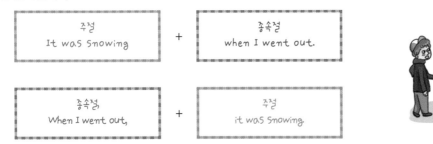

It was snowing **when** I went out.

= **When** I went out, it was snowing. 내가 밖으로 나갔을 때, 눈이 오고 있었다.

* 주절과 종속절을 이어주는 접속사로, 종속접속사가 이끄는 절은 주절의 앞이나 뒤에 올 수 있다.
종속절이 주절의 앞에 오는 경우에는 종속절의 끝에 쉼표(,)가 들어간다.

❷ when (～할 때): 시간을 나타내는 절을 이끈다.

My mother was cooking **when** I came home. 내가 집에 왔을 때 어머니는 요리하고 있었다.

When I went into her room, she was sleeping. 내가 그녀의 방에 들어갔을 때, 그녀는 자고 있었다.

When David was in Australia, he saw a cute koala. David는 호주에 있었을 때 귀여운 코알라를 보았다.

❸ before (～하기 전에): 시간을 나타내는 절을 이끈다.

I want to see Jennifer **before** she goes abroad. 나는 Jennifer가 해외에 가기 전에 그녀를 보기를 원한다.

Turn off the light **before** you go to bed. 잠자리에 들기 전에 불을 꺼라.

Before it gets dark, I should go home. 어두워지기 전에 나는 집에 가야 한다.

❹ after (～한 후에): 시간을 나타내는 절을 이끈다.

After I did my homework, I wrote my diary. 나는 숙제를 끝내고 나서 일기를 썼다.

Let's go to the movies **after** we eat lunch. 점심을 먹은 후에 영화 보러 가자.

Can I borrow the book **after** you read it? 네가 그 책을 읽고 나서 내가 그 책을 빌려도 될까?

❺ because (～이기 때문에): 원인이나 이유를 나타내는 절을 이끈다.

I was absent from school **because** I was sick. 나는 아팠기 때문에 학교에 결석했다.

Because it was cold, I turned on the heater. 추웠기 때문에 나는 히터를 틀었다.

We didn't say anything **because** she looked angry. 그녀가 화가 나 보였기 때문에 우리는 아무 말도 하지 않았다.

Practice

Answers p.16

A 다음 괄호 안에서 알맞은 것을 고르시오.

1 Call me (when / because) you get home.

2 I can't help you (when / because) I have to go now.

3 I usually take a shower (before / after) I go to school.

4 Don't forget to close the window (before / after) you go out.

5 What do you usually do (when / before) you have free time?

6 (After / Because) he was hungry, he ordered two hamburgers.

7 I can play tennis with you (after / because) I finish my homework.

> **plus**
>
> 종속접속사 when은 '~할 때'의 뜻으로, 「when+주어+동사」의 어순으로 쓴다.
> When I'm at home, I usually sleep.
> 나는 집에 있을 때 주로 잔다.
>
> 의문사 when은 '언제'라는 뜻으로, 「when+동사+주어 ~?」의 어순으로 쓰인다.
> When did you meet her?
> 너는 언제 그녀를 만났니?

B 다음 우리말과 같은 뜻이 되도록 문장을 완성하시오.

1 Daniel은 한국에 오기 전에 한국어를 배웠다.

  → _____ Daniel came to Korea, he learned Korean.

2 비가 내려서 나는 약속을 취소했다.

  → I canceled the appointment _____ it rained.

3 그는 대학에 입학하고 나서 뉴욕으로 이사했다.

  → _____ he entered college, he moved to New York.

4 Sue는 런던에 있었을 때 이모 댁에서 머물렀다.

  → _____ Sue was in London, she stayed with her aunt.

5 엄마가 집에 오시기 전에 나는 방을 청소했다.

  → I cleaned my room _____ my mother came home.

C 다음 우리말과 같은 뜻이 되도록 주어진 단어를 배열하여 문장을 완성하시오.

1 Becky는 저녁을 먹고 나서 잠이 들었다. (after, dinner, had, she)

  → Becky fell asleep _____.

2 영화가 시작하기 전에 나는 팝콘을 샀다. (started, the movie, before)

  → I bought some popcorn _____.

3 Mike는 내일 시험이 있어서 공부하고 있다. (a test, because, tomorrow, has, he)

  → Mike is studying _____.

> **Eng-Eng VOCA**
>
> | take a shower | to wash your body with water and soap |
> |---|---|
> | cancel | to decide that a planned event will not happen |
> | appointment | an agreement to meet with someone at a particular time |
> | enter | to start studying at a school or university |
> | fall asleep | to begin sleeping |

Grammar
Lesson 3

★ 시간을 나타내는 전치사

in	~에	in 2010, in winter, in January, in the morning
on		on January 1st, on Monday, on Christmas Day
at		at seven o'clock, at night, at noon
during	~동안	during the vacation, during the summer
for		for a year, for a month, for an hour, for a minute
until	~까지	until Thursday, until January, until midnight
by		by Thursday, by January, by the end of this week

❶ in: 하루의 때(오전, 오후 등), 월, 계절, 연도 등 비교적 긴 시간 앞에 쓴다.

Emily has two classes in the afternoon. Emily는 오후에 수업이 두 개 있다.
She will graduate in February. 그녀는 2월에 졸업할 것이다.
We went to Tokyo in 2016. 우리는 2016년에 도쿄에 갔다.

❷ on: 날짜, 요일, 특정한 날 등의 앞에 쓴다.

I was born on September 6th, 2005. 나는 2005년 9월 6일에 태어났다.
We have a test on Monday. 우리는 월요일에 시험이 있다.
People eat turkey on Thanksgiving Day. 사람들은 추수감사절에 칠면조를 먹는다.

❸ at: 구체적인 시간이나 특정 시점 앞에 쓴다.

Let's meet at five o'clock. 다섯 시 정각에 만나자.
I usually eat lunch at noon. 나는 주로 정오에 점심을 먹는다.

❹ during, for (~ 동안)

My father is going to Paris during the vacation. 아버지는 휴가 동안 파리에 갈 것이다.
Jimmy was in the hospital during the winter. Jimmy는 겨울 동안 병원에 입원했다.

He will be absent for five days. 그는 5일 동안 결석할 것이다.
I talked to her on the phone for thirty minutes. 나는 30분 동안 전화로 그녀와 얘기했다.

* during은 특정한 기간을 나타내는 명사 앞에, for는 구체적인 숫자 앞에 쓴다.

❺ by, until (~까지)

We have to finish our report by next Monday. 우리는 보고서를 다음 주 월요일까지 끝내야 한다.
We are on holiday until next Friday. 우리는 다음 주 금요일까지 휴가다.

* by는 일회성으로 동작이나 상태가 완료되는 것을 의미하는 반면, until은 계속되던 행동이나 상태가 완료되는 것을 의미한다.

Practice

Answers p.16

A 다음 빈칸에 in, on, at 중 알맞은 것을 써 넣으시오.

1 _____ Wednesday

2 _____ New Year's Day

3 _____ December 25th

4 _____ 2:30 in the morning

5 _____ spring

6 _____ 2017

7 _____ night

8 _____ the afternoon

9 _____ the end of the day

10 _____ three o'clock

B 다음 괄호 안에서 알맞은 것을 고르시오.

1 My grandfather died (in / on) 2016.

2 He will travel (during / for) a week.

3 She'll stay here (until / by) next month.

4 Mrs. Jefferson always drives carefully (at / in) night.

5 We'll invite Edward for dinner (in / on) Saturday.

6 Don't talk with your friends (during / for) the class.

7 We should finish our homework (until / by) five o'clock.

C 다음 우리말과 같은 뜻이 되도록 문장을 완성하시오.

1 여름에는 날씨가 덥고 습하다.

→ It is hot and humid _____ summer.

2 수업은 아홉 시에 시작할 것이다.

→ The class will begin _____ nine o'clock.

3 나는 오후 다섯 시까지 도서관에서 공부할 것이다.

→ I'll study at the library _____ 5:00 p.m.

4 Rachel은 대개 아침에 늦게 일어난다.

→ Rachel usually gets up late _____ the morning.

5 Jenny는 목요일에 피아노 강습을 받을 것이다.

→ Jenny will take a piano lesson _____ Thursday.

Eng-Eng VOCA

spring	the season between winter and summer when leaves and flowers appear
travel	to go from one place to another
stay	to be in the same place for a period of time
invite	to ask someone to come to a party, wedding, meal, etc.
lesson	an activity that you do to learn something

Grammar
Lesson 4

★ 장소를 나타내는 전치사

A girl is sitting **at** her desk.
The bed is **behind** the desk.
The box is **beside** the bed.
The toys are **in** the box.

The cat is **under** the bed.
The bag is **on** the bed.
The clock is **on** the wall.
The bookshelf is **over** the bed.

▷ 장소를 나타내는 전치사의 종류와 쓰임

in	~ 안에 (들어갈 수 있는 공간, 넓은 장소)	in a room, in the country, in China
at	~에 (지점, 좁은 장소)	at the bus stop, at my desk, at school, at the corner
on	~ 위에 (표면과 접촉)	on the floor, on the wall, on the table
over	~ 위에 (표면과 떨어져)	over the mountain, over the river
under	~ 아래에 (표면과 떨어져)	under the bridge, under the table
beside	~ 옆에	beside the bed, beside the car
behind	~ 뒤에	behind the door, behind the bus

We have many flowers **in the garden.** 정원에 꽃이 많이 있다.

Turn left **at the corner.** 모퉁이에서 좌회전하시오.

There are many paintings **on the wall.** 벽에 그림들이 많이 있다.

A plane is flying **over the town.** 비행기 한 대가 마을 위로 날아가고 있다.

A puppy is sleeping **under the table.** 강아지 한 마리가 테이블 아래에서 자고 있다.

There is a pretty girl **beside Jim.** Jim 옆에 한 예쁜 소녀가 있다.

There is a tree **behind the old building.** 그 오래된 건물 뒤에 나무 한 그루가 있다.

Practice

Answers p.16

A 다음 그림을 보고 〈보기〉에서 알맞은 전치사를 골라 문장을 완성하시오.

> **보기**   in   under   beside   on

1 The vase is _____ the table.

2 The flowers are _____ the vase.

3 The dog is _____ the table.

4 The ball is _____ the dog.

B 다음 괄호 안에서 알맞은 것을 고르시오.

1 There are many fish (in / at) the river.

2 I dropped a book (behind / on) the floor.

3 There is some coffee (over / in) the cup.

4 There is an old bridge (on / over) the river.

5 I arrived (in / at) the airport at seven o'clock.

6 They were playing games (over / at) the beach.

7 My sister is living (in / at) San Francisco now.

8 I didn't buy this (at / on) the shop. I bought it online.

C 다음 우리말과 같은 뜻이 되도록 빈칸에 알맞은 전치사를 쓰시오.

> **Hint**
>
> 〈기타 전치사〉
> between A and B
> A와 B 사이에
> across from
> ~의 맞은편에
> in front of
> ~의 앞에(↔ behind)
> next to
> ~의 옆에(= beside)

1 나무 아래에 꽃이 조금 있다.

→ There are some flowers _____ the tree.

2 우리집 개는 항상 내 옆에 앉는다.

→ My dog always sits _____ _____ me.

3 한국과 일본 사이에는 동해가 있다.

→ There is the East Sea _____ Korea _____ Japan.

4 문 앞에 신문이 있다.

→ There is a newspaper _____ _____ _____ the door.

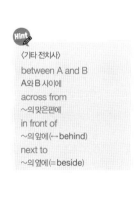

Eng-Eng VOCA

drop	to let something fall; to fall
floor	the flat surface that you stand on
arrive	to come to a place after traveling
airport	a place where planes land and take off
online	while connected to a computer or the Internet

VOCA
in Grammar

Answers p.17

A 다음 주어진 단어에 빈칸에 공통으로 들어갈 수 있는 것끼리 바르게 연결하시오.

1 on •

2 in •

3 at •

4 behind •

5 under •

a. ____ the curtain, ____ schedule

b. ____ the wall, ____ Saturday

c. ____ the tree, children aged 13 and ____

d. ____ noon, ____ the bus stop

e. ____ the drawer, ____ March

B 다음 괄호 안에서 알맞은 것을 고르시오.

1 Jack lost his glasses, (but / so) he couldn't see anything.

2 We played games (and / but) sang songs.

3 (After / When) I did my homework, I wrote my diary.

4 Can I borrow the book (after / when) you read it?

5 We didn't say anything (because / before) she looked angry.

C 다음 〈보기〉에서 알맞은 단어를 골라 문장을 완성하시오.

보기	for	during	until	by	over

1 A plane is flying _____ the town.

2 We have to finish our report _____ next Monday.

3 We are on holiday _____ next Friday.

4 Jimmy was in the hospital _____ the winter.

5 I talked to her on the phone _____ thirty minutes.

WORKBOOK

A 다음 빈칸에 적절한 be동사의 현재형을 쓰시오.

1 You _____ the best players.

2 We _____ in the same class.

3 It _____ my backpack.

4 I _____ a baseball player.

5 They _____ my parents.

6 She _____ at school.

B 다음 밑줄 친 부분을 줄여서 문장을 다시 쓰시오.

1 It is my purse. → _____

2 You are a good student. → _____

3 He is at the library. → _____

4 We are good at English. → _____

5 I am in the kitchen. → _____

C 다음 〈보기〉에서 알맞은 be동사를 골라 문장을 완성하시오. (중복 가능)

보기   am   are   is   was   were

1 I _____ hungry now. I _____ very full an hour ago.

2 They _____ actors now. They _____ soccer players before.

3 Two years ago, he _____ in Japan. Now, he _____ in Korea.

4 You _____ sick last night, but today you _____ fine.

D 다음 우리말과 일치하도록 괄호에 주어진 말을 이용하여 영작하시오.

1 나는 사진작가이다. (I, a photographer)

→ _____

2 그들은 학교에서 인기가 많다. (popular, at school)

→ _____

3 Linda는 발레 무용수이다. (Linda, a ballet dancer)

→ _____

4 나는 어제 온종일 집에 있었다. (at home, all day yesterday)

→ _____

5 우리는 여행 후에 매우 피곤했다. (tired, after the trip)

→ _____

A 다음 밑줄 친 부분의 축약형을 쓰시오.

1 This <u>is not</u> a pen. _____

2 We <u>are not</u> from Germany. _____

3 She <u>was not</u> a jazz singer. _____

4 They <u>were not</u> on the bus. _____

B 다음 주어진 문장을 의문문으로 다시 쓰시오.

1 You are 13 years old. → _____

2 The store was open yesterday. → _____

3 He is Tom's cousin. → _____

4 They were at the airport. → _____

C 다음 대화를 문맥에 맞게 빈칸을 채워 완성하시오. (Yes/No를 이용하되, 빈칸 개수에 맞춰 쓸 것)

1 A: Am I fat?
   B: _____ _____ _____.
      You're thin.

2 A: Are you a teacher?
   B: _____ _____ _____.
      I teach music.

3 A: Is he a wrestler?
   B: _____ _____ _____.
      He is a swimmer.

4 A: Was Jane a popular singer?
   B: _____ _____ _____.
      She had a lot of fans.

5 A: Was it rainy in Tokyo yesterday?
   B: _____ _____ _____.
      It was sunny.

6 A: Were they late for school?
   B: _____ _____ _____.
      They were on time.

D 다음 우리말과 일치하도록 괄호에 주어진 말을 이용하여 영작하시오. (부정문은 축약형을 쓸 것)

1 저것은 사탕가게가 아니다. (that, a candy shop)

   → _____

2 그는 코미디언이 아니었다. (a comedian)

   → _____

3 그들은 그녀의 부모님인가요? (her parents)

   → _____

4 제가 틀린가요? (wrong)

   → _____

A 다음 인칭대명사 표를 완성하시오.

단·복수	주격	소유격	목적격	소유대명사
단수	I			
	you			
	he			
	she			
	it			
복수	we			
	you			
	they			

B 다음 밑줄 친 부분을 적절한 인칭대명사로 바꿔 다시 쓰시오.

1 This is Julie's painting. That is also Julie's.

→ This is _____ painting. That is also _____.

2 Jessy and Mark are very funny. Everybody likes Jessy and Mark.

→ _____ are very funny. Everybody likes _____.

3 John is my best friend. John's hobby is reading books.

→ _____ is my best friend. _____ hobby is reading books.

C 다음 대화문의 밑줄 친 부분 중 잘못된 것을 찾아 고쳐 쓰시오.

A: What's your name?

B: ⓐ My name is Minsu. What's ⓑ your name?

A: My name is Peggy. Nice to meet you.

B: Where are you from?

A: ⓒ I'm from Canada. My father is Korean, and my mother is from Canada.
ⓓ We speak Korean and English at home.

B: That's cool! Do you have any brothers or sisters?

A: I have a little sister. ⓔ She is two years old. I like ⓕ hers!

_____ → _____

A 다음 빈칸에 there, be동사를 이용하여 긍정문 또는 의문문을 완성하시오. (현재형으로 쓸 것)

1 _____ _____ a bank on the corner.　3 _____ _____ a drugstore in your town?

2 _____ _____ some kids in the pool.　4 _____ _____ many dishes in the sink?

B 다음 주어진 문장을 괄호 안의 조건대로 바꿔 쓰시오.

1 There is a bag in his locker. (의문문)

→ _____

2 There are books on the shelf. (의문문)

→ _____

3 There is a bear in the cage. (부정문)

→ _____

4 There are many books in my room. (부정문)

→ _____

C 다음 그림을 보고 각 물음에 대한 대답을 완성하시오. (Yes/No를 이용해서 대답할 것)

1 A: Is there a keyboard on the desk?

B: _____

2 A: Are there some pencils in the cup?

B: _____

3 A: Are there some houses in the picture?

B: _____

4 A: How many books are there on the desk?

B: _____

D 다음 우리말과 일치하도록 괄호에 주어진 말을 배열하여 영작하시오.

1 지하에 쥐가 있니? (a mouse, is, in the basement, there)

→ _____

2 바구니에 쿠키가 조금 있다. (some cookies, there, in the basket, are)

→ _____

3 교실에는 학생이 몇 명이 있나요? (many, students, there, how, in the classroom, are)

→ _____

Ⓐ 다음 주어진 동사의 3인칭 단수 현재형을 쓰시오.

1 close _____		*5* catch _____		*9* try _____	
2 want _____		*6* pass _____		*10* carry _____	
3 go _____		*7* wash _____		*11* buy _____	
4 do _____		*8* mix _____		*12* have _____	

Ⓑ 다음 주어진 동사의 현재형을 이용하여 문장을 완성하시오.

1 I _____ snacks at the supermarket. (buy)

2 My sister _____ cats and dogs. (love)

3 Brian _____ tennis after school. (play)

4 He _____ his hair in the morning. (wash)

5 We _____ singing together. (enjoy)

6 Evan and Ian _____ shopping together. (go)

7 Ants _____ six legs. (have)

8 They _____ in a big house. (live)

9 You _____ really fast. (speak)

10 She _____ your e-mail address. (know)

Ⓒ 다음 우리말과 일치하도록 괄호에 주어진 말을 이용하여 영작하시오.

1 그녀는 매일 세수를 한다. (wash, her face, every day)

→ _____

2 우리는 액션 영화를 좋아한다. (like, action movies)

→ _____

3 우리 학교는 9시 정각에 시작한다. (my school, start)

→ _____

4 곰은 겨울 동안 동굴 안에서 잠을 잔다. (bears, sleep, in the cave, during the winter)

→ _____

6 Ron과 그의 동생은 주말마다 체스를 둔다. (Ron and his brother, play, on weekends)

→ _____

Ⓐ 다음 괄호에 주어진 말을 이용하여 문장을 완성하시오. (현재형을 쓸 것)

1 I _____ a lie. (not, tell)

2 She _____ early. (not, get up)

3 Lisa _____ camping every weekend. (not, go)

4 They _____ across the street. (not, run)

5 Your cat _____ bad. (not, smell)

Ⓑ 다음 주어진 문장을 의문문으로 다시 쓰시오.

1 We have math class today.

→ _____

2 She studies English every day.

→ _____

3 Ashley eats junk food.

→ _____

4 Tigers have stripes.

→ _____

5 You and Isabella read many books.

→ _____

Ⓒ 다음 표를 보고 물음에 대한 대답을 완성하시오. (Yes/No를 이용하되, 빈칸 개수에 맞춰 쓸 것)

	Saturday	Sunday
Paul	practice the piano	clean the house
Andy and Brian	go to the gym	play soccer

1 A: Does Paul practice the violin on Saturday?   B: _____ _____ _____ .

2 A: Do Andy and Brian go to the gym on Saturday? B: _____ _____ _____ .

3 A: Does Paul clean the house on Sunday?   B: _____ _____ _____ .

4 A: Do Andy and Brian play baseball on Sunday?   B: _____ _____ _____ .

A 다음 주어진 동사의 과거형을 쓰시오.

1 end	_____	5 think	_____	9 do	_____
2 arrive	_____	6 go	_____	10 put	_____
3 try	_____	7 have	_____	11 read	_____
4 drop	_____	8 buy	_____	12 spend	_____

B 다음 괄호에 주어진 동사를 이용하여 과거형 문장을 완성하시오.

1 I _____ the test yesterday. (pass)

2 My father _____ his car last year. (sell)

3 His sisters _____ to the movies last Friday. (go)

4 Mr. White _____ us math last month. (teach)

5 He _____ a book a week ago. (read)

C 다음 주어진 문장을 괄호 안의 조건대로 바꿔 쓰시오.

1 Sally skipped breakfast this morning. (의문문)

→ _____

2 Ryan got on the train last night. (부정문)

→ _____

3 My father went to work last Saturday. (부정문)

→ _____

4 You bought a new jacket at the mall. (의문문)

→ _____

D 다음 Jack이 어제 한 일과 하지 않은 일에 대해 표를 보고 물음과 답을 완성하시오.

Jack이 어제 한 일		Jack이 어제 하지 않은 일	
clean his room	do his homework	go jogging	watch a movie

1 A: _____   3 A: _____

   B: _____   B: _____

2 A: _____   4 A: _____

   B: _____   B: _____

A 다음 괄호에 주어진 동사를 이용하여 어법에 맞게 현재시제 또는 과거시제로 고쳐 쓰시오.

1 It _____ last night. (rain)

2 He _____ thirsty now. (feel)

3 A dragon fly _____ four wings. (have)

4 They _____ back in 2016. (come)

5 The moon _____ around the Earth. (go)

6 I _____ an exam yesterday. (take)

B 다음 우리말과 일치하도록 괄호에 주어진 말을 이용하여 영작하시오.

1 Sandy는 5분 전에 버스를 놓쳤다. (miss, the bus, five minutes ago)

→ _____

2 Peter는 지난달에 드라마 클럽에 가입했다. (join, the drama club, last month)

→ _____

3 그녀는 매일 축구 연습을 한다. (practice soccer, every day)

→ _____

4 우리 오빠는 생선을 먹지 않는다. (my brother, not, eat, fish)

→ _____

5 Paul은 지난여름에 할머니댁을 방문하지 않았다. (not, visit, his grandmother, last summer)

→ _____

C 다음 미나의 작년과 현재 상황을 나타낸 표를 보고 빈칸을 채워 글을 완성하시오.

	작년	현재
Mina	high school student	college student
	wear a uniform at school	wear casual clothes in college
	live with her family	live alone in Seoul

Mina is my cousin. She ⓐ _____ a high school student last year. She
ⓑ _____ a uniform at school and ⓒ _____ with her family. But she
ⓓ _____ a college student now. She ⓔ _____ casual clothes in college.
And she doesn't live with her family. Her college is in Seoul, so she ⓕ _____
alone in Seoul now.

Ⓐ 다음 주어진 동사의 -ing형을 쓰시오.

1 work _____
2 look _____
3 see _____
4 ride _____

5 take _____
6 have _____
7 hit _____
8 cut _____

9 swim _____
10 run _____
11 lie _____
12 die _____

Ⓑ 다음 괄호에 주어진 동사를 이용하여 어법에 맞게 진행형 문장을 완성하시오.

1 I _____ next to Tom now. (sit)

2 Matt _____ a nap now. (take)

3 Some children _____ bicycles now. (ride)

4 My grandmother _____ her roses at that time. (water)

5 Some people _____ at the park at 9 this morning. (jog)

Ⓒ 다음 주어진 문장을 괄호 안의 조건대로 바꿔 쓰시오. (부정문은 축약형을 쓸 것)

1 They are watching a movie now. (의문문)

→ _____

2 He is waiting for his friends. (의문문)

→ _____

3 The escalator is working now. (부정문)

→ _____

4 We were playing games at 6. (부정문)

→ _____

Ⓓ 다음 괄호에 주어진 말을 이용하여 ⓐ, ⓑ에 들어갈 말을 완성하시오.

Jessica: Hi, Patrick. Did you see Gary? I called him at 8 p.m. yesterday, but he wasn't at home.

Patrick: At that time, ⓐ _____ (he, do) his homework at my place. He left at 9 p.m. By the way, why ⓑ _____ (you, look) for him?

Jessica: He borrowed my notebook last week. He didn't give it back to me.

Ⓐ 다음 우리말에 맞게 〈보기〉에서 알맞은 말을 골라 문장을 완성하시오. (복수 정답 가능)

> **보기**   can   could   may   able to

1 나는 기타를 칠 수 있다. → I _____ play the guitar.

2 그는 프랑스어를 말할 수 있다. → He is _____ speak French.

3 창문을 닫아주시겠어요? → _____ you close the window?

4 그는 오늘 늦을지도 모른다. → He _____ be late today.

5 그녀는 내 전화번호가 없을지도 모른다. → She _____ not have my phone number.

6 당신은 그 방에 들어가면 안 됩니다. → You _____ not enter the room.

Ⓑ 다음 주어진 문장을 be able to를 이용해서 다시 쓰시오.

1 My uncle can drive a bus. → _____

2 I cannot solve the problem. → _____

3 He couldn't answer the question. → _____

4 Can you fix the computer? → _____

5 They could dive in the sea. → _____

6 Could she solve the problem? → _____

Ⓒ 다음 우리말과 일치하도록 괄호에 주어진 말을 배열하여 영작하시오.

1 그는 매우 부자일지도 모른다. (very rich, he, be, may)

→ _____

2 나 물 좀 마셔도 될까? (have, I, can, some water)

→ _____

3 Dennis는 춤을 매우 잘 출 수 있다. (able, is, Dennis, to, dance, very well)

→ _____

4 그들은 출구를 찾을 수 없었다. (were, able, they, to, find, not, an exit)

→ _____

5 당신은 지금 방을 나가면 안 됩니다. (the room, you, may, leave, not, now)

→ _____

A 다음 우리말에 맞게 〈보기〉에서 알맞은 말을 골라 문장을 완성하시오. (복수 정답 가능)

> **보기**   must   must not   have to   don't have to   had to

1 그들은 규칙을 따라야만 한다.

→ They _____ follow the rules.

2 당신은 여기서 사진을 찍으면 안 된다.

→ You _____ take pictures here.

3 그는 피곤한 것이 틀림없다.

→ He _____ be tired.

4 나는 오늘까지 그 일을 끝낼 필요가 없다.

→ I _____ finish the work today.

5 우리는 어제 택시를 타고 집에 가야 했다.

→ We _____ take a taxi home yesterday.

B 다음 괄호에 주어진 말을 이용하여 조언하는 문장을 완성하시오. (should/shouldn't를 추가할 것)

1 You look tired. You _____. (take a rest)

2 You _____. (eat too much junk food)

3 You have a bad cold. You _____. (see a doctor)

4 You _____ in this cold weather. (stay outside too long)

C 다음 주어진 문장을 have to를 이용해서 다시 쓰시오.

1 You must eat a lot of vegetables.

→ _____

2 She must arrive home by twelve o'clock.

→ _____

3 He must do his homework by today.

→ _____

4 Must I finish my work today?

→ _____

A 다음 괄호에 주어진 말을 이용하여 미래 의미의 문장을 완성하시오.

1 She _____ to London next September. (will, go)

2 I'm sorry. I _____ late again. (won't)

3 _____ you _____ by my office this afternoon? (will, drop)

4 They _____ in the event. (going, participate)

5 He _____ his uncle next week. (not, going, visit)

6 _____ it _____ tomorrow? (going, rain)

B 다음 주어진 문장을 괄호 안의 조건대로 바꿔 쓰시오.

1 She is going to sing at the party. (부정문)

→ _____

2 They are going to take piano lessons. (의문문)

→ _____

3 Tim and Susie will eat out this evening. (be going to를 이용)

→ _____

4 He will leave for Toronto tomorrow. (be going to를 이용)

→ _____

5 Mark will learn taekwondo starting from next month. (의문문, be going to를 이용)

→ _____

C 다음 괄호에 주어진 말을 이용하여 ⓐ~ⓔ에 들어갈 말을 완성하시오.

Sally: Peggy and I are ⓐ _____ (watch) the new movie this Saturday. ⓑ _____ (will, join) us?

Kathy: I am sorry but I have some other plans. I'm ⓒ _____ (buy) a present for Lisa. Her birthday is next week.

Sally: So, are ⓓ _____ (you, to go) to her birthday party?

Kathy: Yes, I am. I'm very excited.

Sally: How about this Sunday? Do you have any plans?

Kathy: I'm ⓔ _____ (take) my dog to the vet. He is sick.

A 다음 주어진 명사의 복수형을 쓰시오.

1 key _____

2 piano _____

3 bench _____

4 church _____

5 factory _____

6 city _____

7 life _____

8 wolf _____

9 foot _____

10 mouse _____

11 deer _____

12 fish _____

B 다음 괄호에 주어진 명사를 알맞은 형태로 바꿔 문장을 완성하시오.

1 He traveled in many _____. (country)

2 The shepherd has fifteen _____ on the farm. (sheep)

3 He has a lot of _____ today. (homework)

4 I have two little _____. (sister)

5 Mr. Anderson has three _____. (child)

6 I brush my _____ three times a day. (tooth)

C 다음 우리말과 일치하도록 괄호에 주어진 말을 이용하여 영작하시오.

1 나는 돈이 많지 않다. (not, have, much, money)

→ _____

2 바구니에 토마토가 세 개 있다. (there, three, tomato, in the basket)

→ _____

3 그는 사전을 두 개 가지고 있다. (have, two, dictionary)

→ _____

4 우리는 소금이 약간 필요하다. (need, some, salt)

→ _____

5 많은 사슴들이 숲에 살고 있다. (many, deer, live, in the forest)

→ _____

6 이 아름다운 나뭇잎들의 사진들을 찍어라. (take, picture, of, these, beautiful, leaf)

→ _____

A 다음 빈칸에 a와 an 중 알맞은 것을 쓰시오.

1 _____ horse

2 _____ boy

3 _____ desk

4 _____ artist

5 _____ umbrella

6 _____ orange

7 _____ animal

8 _____ egg

9 _____ useful tool

10 _____ window

11 _____ truck

12 _____ university

13 _____ scientist

14 _____ hour

15 _____ honest student

B 다음 빈칸에 a(n) 또는 the를 쓰고, 필요 없는 경우 X표 하시오.

1 He is _____ soccer player.

2 There's _____ MP3 file in this folder.

3 She plays _____ tennis every day.

4 _____ sun is rising.

5 I met a boy. _____ boy was kind.

6 Tim bought _____ black jacket.

7 Mr. Kim is _____ English teacher.

8 He came here by _____ train.

9 Paul went to _____ school.

10 Can you close _____ door?

C 다음 우리말과 일치하도록 괄호에 주어진 말을 이용하여 영작하시오. (필요한 경우, 적절한 관사를 쓸 것)

1 Tim은 10시에 잠자러 간다. (go, bed, at 10)

→ _____

2 Mary는 밴드에서 기타를 연주한다. (play, guitar, in the band)

→ _____

3 하늘에 있는 달을 봐라. (look at, moon, in, sky)

→ _____

4 내가 가장 좋아하는 과목은 음악이다. (my favorite subject, music)

→ _____

5 그의 아버지는 기차를 타고 출근하신다. (my father, go, work, train)

→ _____

6 Jenny는 한 달에 두 번 조부모님댁을 방문한다. (visit, her grandparents, twice, month)

→ _____

A 다음 우리말에 맞게 this, that, these, those를 써서 문장을 완성하시오.

1 이것은 내 교과서야.

→ _____ is my textbook.

2 이 개들을 봐라.

→ Look at _____ puppies.

3 Jeremy는 저 그림을 정말 좋아한다.

→ Jeremy likes _____ painting a lot.

4 나는 지난주에 저 청바지를 샀다.

→ I bought _____ jeans last week.

5 이분들은 나의 부모님이십니다.

→ _____ are my parents.

6 우리 언니는 저것들과 같은 것 하나를 집에 갖고 있어.

→ My sister has one of _____ at home.

B 다음 빈칸에 one, ones, it 중 알맞은 것을 써서 문장을 완성하시오.

1 Where is my notebook computer? I need _____ now.

2 These shorts are too big. Do you have smaller _____?

3 Peter is wearing a nice jacket. I want a similar _____.

4 Mrs. Park bought a new car. She will sell her old _____.

5 Jim lost his watch yesterday. He's still looking for _____.

C 다음 괄호에 주어진 말을 이용하여 어법에 맞게 문장을 완성하시오. (동사는 현재형을 쓸 것)

1 All _____ _____ not alike. (teenager, be)

2 Each _____ _____ its own national flag. (country, have)

3 All of the _____ _____ middle school students. (girl, be)

4 Each _____ _____ different. (person, look)

5 Every _____ _____ his or her own locker. (student, have)

Ⓐ 다음 괄호에 주어진 단어와 비인칭 주어를 이용하여 대화를 완성하시오. (축약형을 쓸 것)

1 A: What day is it today? (Saturday)

B: _____

2 A: What time is it now? (8:40)

B: _____

3 A: What date is it today? (October 3rd)

B: _____

4 A: How's the weather today? (sunny)

B: _____

Ⓑ 다음 우리말과 일치하도록 괄호에 주어진 말을 배열하여 영작하시오.

1 여기서 시청까지 거리가 얼마나 되나요? (is, how far, from here, it, to City Hall)

→ _____

2 너의 집에서 학교까지 얼마나 머니? (does, how long, it, from your house, take, to school)

→ _____

3 버스로 세 시간 걸린다. (three hours, takes, by bus, it)

→ _____

4 여기 안은 왜 이렇게 어둡나요? (in here, why, so dark, it, is)

→ _____

Ⓒ 다음 ⓐ와 ⓑ의 우리말과 일치하도록 괄호에 주어진 말을 이용하여 문장을 완성하시오.

Peter: What do I need to bring for the test tomorrow?

Julia: Each person needs a piece of paper and a pen.

Peter: ⓐ 시험을 치르는 것은 얼마나 오래 걸려?

Julia: ⓑ 약 두 시간 정도 걸려.

Peter: I see. Thank you.

ⓐ _____ (long, take, do the test)

ⓑ _____ (will, take, about two hours)

A 다음 괄호에 주어진 형용사가 들어갈 위치에 V표 하시오.

1 Andy is wearing a coat. (warm)

2 I found a photo in the drawer. (beautiful)

3 She needs to drink something. (hot)

4 Did he ask for anything? (special)

5 There are trees along the river. (tall)

B 다음 우리말에 맞게 〈보기〉에서 알맞은 말을 골라 문장을 완성하시오. (복수 정답 가능)

보기   many   much

1 I saw _____ singers at the music festival.

2 My English teacher doesn't give us _____ homework.

보기   few   little

3 There was _____ milk in the bottle.

4 There were _____ people in the park.

보기   a few   a little

5 I sent _____ letters to my friend.

6 Here's _____ information about the test.

C 다음 우리말과 같은 뜻이 되도록 주어진 단어와 some이나 any를 이용하여 영작하시오.

1 벽에 그림 몇 점이 있다. (there, pictures, on the wall)

→ _____

2 차 좀 드시겠어요? (would, like, tea)

→ _____

3 내 지갑에는 돈이 하나도 없다. (there, money, in my wallet)

→ _____

4 당신은 여기서 사진을 한 장도 찍을 수 없습니다. (cannot, take, pictures, here)

→ _____

Ⓐ 다음 주어진 형용사의 부사 형태를 쓰시오.

1 quiet _____

2 happy _____

3 terrible _____

4 lucky _____

5 simple _____

6 real _____

7 careful _____

8 nice _____

9 main _____

10 new _____

11 good _____

12 fast _____

13 necessary _____

14 comfortable _____

15 heavy _____

16 bad _____

17 slow _____

18 possible _____

19 early _____

20 special _____

Ⓑ 다음 괄호 안에 주어진 단어를 알맞은 곳에 각각 써넣으시오.

1 He swims very _____. He is a _____ swimmer. (good, well)

2 Mr. Kang is very _____. He always talks _____. (quiet, quietly)

3 Emily is a _____ learner. She learns very _____. (quick, quickly)

4 Angela is a _____ kid. Look! She is playing _____. (happy, happily)

Ⓒ 다음 괄호에 주어진 단어를 문장의 적절한 위치에 넣어 다시 쓰시오.

1 They eat out for dinner. (sometimes)

→ _____

2 Tom gets good grades. (often)

→ _____

3 Susie is late for school. (never)

→ _____

4 Brad gets up early. (usually)

→ _____

5 You should wear your seatbelt. (always)

→ _____

A 다음 주어진 형용사의 비교급, 최상급을 쓰시오.

1 cheap _____ _____

2 simple _____ _____

3 hot _____ _____

4 lucky _____ _____

5 curious _____ _____

6 bad _____ _____

7 good _____ _____

8 much _____ _____

9 far(더욱) _____ _____

10 far(먼) _____ _____

B 다음 괄호에 주어진 단어의 비교급과 최상급을 이용하여 문장을 완성하시오.

1 Mike arrived _____ than Meg, but Bob arrived _____ of all. (early)

2 Jerry is _____ than Tom, but Sam is _____ student here. (smart)

3 Danny is _____ than Brad, but Hailey is _____ in school. (heavy)

4 Mom sings _____ than me, but Dad sings _____ in my family. (well)

C 다음 〈보기〉에 주어진 말을 이용하여 ⓐ~ⓒ를 채우시오. (필요하면 어형을 변화시킬 것)

| 보기 | popular | dark | large |

A: I'd like to buy a jacket. Do you have anything good?

B: How about this white jacket?

A: Well, that is too bright. I want something ⓐ _____.

B: We have some black jackets, and we also have brown jackets.

A: Which one is more popular?

B: The black ones are as ⓑ _____ as the brown ones.

A: I think those are too tight. Do you have a ⓒ _____ one?

B: Of course, we do. What size do you wear?

A: A medium size will be better for me.

A 다음 괄호에 주어진 말을 이용하여 문장을 완성하시오. (to부정사를 쓸 것)

1 나는 새 신발을 사고 싶다. (want, buy)

→ I _____ new shoes.

2 그는 무서운 영화 보는 것을 좋아한다. (like, watch)

→ He _____ horror movies.

3 프랑스어를 배우는 것은 재미있다. (learn)

→ _____ French is fun.

4 액션 영화를 보는 것은 신이 난다. (watch)

→ _____ action movies is exciting.

5 나의 계획은 일주일 동안 제주도에 머무는 것이다. (stay)

→ My plan is _____ in Jeju for a week.

B 다음 주어진 두 개의 문장을 to부정사를 이용한 문장으로 완성하시오.

1 She will go to the festival. She is happy.

→ She is happy _____.

2 He went to the supermarket. He bought some vegetables.

→ He went to the supermarket _____.

3 I have a book. I will give it to my sister.

→ I have a book _____.

4 Paul wanted to be a pianist. So he practiced hard.

→ Paul practiced hard _____.

C 다음 우리말과 일치하도록 괄호에 주어진 말을 배열하여 영작하시오.

1 서울은 방문하기 좋은 곳이다. (Seoul, visit, a good place, to, is)

→ _____

2 나는 Mike와 저녁을 먹으려고 그에게 전화했다. (Mike, have dinner, I, to, with him, called)

→ _____

3 집에 갈 시간이다. (to, go home, time, it's)

→ _____

4 John은 오늘 할 일이 많다. (a lot of work, has, to, John, do, today)

→ _____

A 다음 괄호에 주어진 동사를 동명사로 바꿔 문장을 완성하시오.

1 Kevin enjoys _____ soccer. (play)

2 Your sister is good at _____ puzzles. (solve)

3 My bad habit is _____ my nails. (bite)

4 Jake's hobby is _____ stamps. (collect)

5 _____ in the river is not easy. (swim)

B 다음 우리말과 일치하도록 괄호에 주어진 말과 동명사를 이용하여 문장을 완성하시오.

1 그녀는 기타 치는 것을 좋아한다. (play, the guitar)

→ She loves _____.

2 규칙적으로 운동하는 것은 당신의 건강에 중요하다. (exercise, regularly)

→ _____ is important for your health.

3 우리 삼촌은 새로운 사업을 시작하는 것에 대해 생각 중이다. (start, a new business)

→ My uncle is thinking about _____.

4 그들이 가장 좋아하는 활동은 사진을 찍는 것이다. (take, photographs)

→ Their favorite activity is _____.

C 다음 우리말과 일치하도록 괄호에 주어진 말을 이용하여 문장을 완성하시오.

1 저를 도와주셔서 감사합니다. (me, help, for)

→ Thank you _____.

2 늦어서 죄송합니다. (sorry for, be late)

→ I'm _____.

3 그녀는 동물 사진 찍는 것을 즐긴다. (enjoy, take pictures of animals)

→ She _____.

4 다른 사람들 앞에서 말하는 것은 어렵다. (speak, in front of, other people, be)

→ _____ difficult.

5 그의 취미는 단편 영화를 만드는 것이다. (is, make, short films)

→ His hobby _____.

A 다음 괄호에 주어진 동사를 이용하여 문장을 완성하시오.

1 My mother enjoys _____. (swim)

2 Do you want _____ my cookies? (try)

3 I hope _____ you soon. (see)

4 He quit _____ at the bank last month. (work)

5 Terry plans _____ London. (visit)

B 다음 우리말과 같은 뜻이 되도록 주어진 단어를 이용하여 문장을 완성하시오.

1 나는 이탈리아 음식이 먹고 싶다. (feel, eat)

→ I _____ Italian food.

2 우리는 그 과제를 하느라 바빴다. (busy, do)

→ We were _____ the project.

3 그들은 게임을 하느라 너무 많은 시간을 보냈다. (spend, too much time, play)

→ They _____ games.

4 Laura 이모는 우리가 그 무서운 영화를 보는 것을 허락하셨다. (let, watch)

→ Aunt Laura _____ the scary movie.

C 다음 대화문을 읽고 물음에 답하시오.

> **Mom:** Fred, wash your hands and have dinner.
>
> **Fred:** Mom, I want ⓐ _____ (eat) pizza. Can I order pizza for delivery?
>
> **Mom:** No. It's 10 o'clock. (a) 피자를 먹기에는 너무 늦었어. It makes you ⓑ _____ (get) fat.
>
> **Fred:** But I like ⓒ _____ (eat) pizza. I'll have just one slice.
>
> **Mom:** How about ⓓ _____ (have) salad now and pizza tomorrow?
>
> **Fred:** Okay.

1 괄호에 주어진 말을 이용하여 ⓐ~ⓓ에 들어갈 말을 완성하시오.

ⓐ _____ ⓑ _____ ⓒ _____ ⓓ _____

2 (a)의 우리말과 일치하도록 주어진 단어를 배열하여 영작하시오. (too, is, to, late, pizza, it, eat)

→ _____

Chapter 8

A 다음 〈보기〉와 같이 주어와 동사를 찾아 밑줄을 긋고, S(주어), V(동사), C(보어)로 표시하시오.

> 보기
>
> Mark is in his room.   Matthew is excited.
> S   V   V   C

1 He is running very fast.

2 The Earth moves around the Sun.

3 The concert will begin soon.

4 The flower smells good.

5 The chair is comfortable.

6 He became a scientist.

7 The soup tastes great.

8 The police officer works really hard.

B 다음 괄호에 주어진 단어를 이용하여 각각의 문장을 완성하시오. (필요하면 어형을 변화할 것)

1 (easy)   • Swimming is _____.
            • He swims _____.

2 (happy)   • They felt _____.
            • They lived _____.

3 (silent) • She kept _____.
            • She sat down _____.

4 (quiet)   • They were _____.
            • I went out _____.

5 (soft)   • Her voice sounds _____.
            • She spoke _____.

6 (beautiful) • Her song is _____.
               • She sings _____.

C 다음 우리말과 일치하도록 괄호에 주어진 말을 배열하여 영작하시오.

1 열차는 10시에 도착한다. (arrives, the train, at 10)

→ _____

2 해가 밝게 빛나고 있다. (is shining, the sun, brightly)

→ _____

3 오늘 아침은 추웠다. (I, cold, felt, this morning)

→ _____

4 이 케이크는 맛이 매우 달다. (tastes, this cake, sweet, very)

→ _____

5 너의 오빠는 매일 지각한다. (every day, your brother, late, is)

→ _____

A 다음 밑줄 친 동사의 목적어를 쓰시오. (경우에 따라 답이 두 개 가능)

1 They <u>saw</u> the moon in the sky. _____

2 The kid <u>wrote</u> a letter to his grandfather. _____

3 An old man <u>asked</u> me for directions. _____

4 Tom <u>passed</u> Jake the ball. _____

5 She <u>told</u> her son a funny story. _____

B 다음 두 문장이 같은 뜻이 되도록 빈칸을 완성하시오. (적절한 전치사를 쓸 것)

1 Mr. Smith sent them a fax yesterday.

= Mr. Smith sent _____ .

2 Tom made his dog a house.

= Tom made _____ .

3 My mother showed me some old photos.

= My mother showed _____ .

4 The teacher asked him a question.

= The teacher asked _____ .

5 She got her husband a nice suit.

= She got _____ .

C 다음 대화문을 읽고 물음에 답하시오.

Monica: Dad, who's cooking in the kitchen?

Father: It's Alex. He is cooking dinner ⓐ _____ Mom. It's her birthday.

Monica: Oh, that sounds great. Mom will be happy. What did you buy
ⓑ _____ her?

Father: I will give a necklace ⓒ _____ her. How about you?

Monica: I bought her a scarf. (a)<u>우리의 선물이 그녀를 행복하게 만들 거예요.</u>

1 ⓐ~ⓒ에 들어갈 전치사를 각각 쓰시오.

ⓐ _____   ⓑ _____   ⓒ _____

2 (a)의 우리말과 일치하도록 주어진 단어를 이용하여 영작하시오. (present, will, make)

→ _____

Ⓐ 다음 괄호에 주어진 말을 이용하여 명령문을 완성하시오.

1 _____ your desk. (clean)

2 _____ nice to your sister. (be)

3 _____ your cell phone before the movie. (turn off)

4 _____ . (not, give up)

5 _____ about it. (not, worry)

6 _____ late again. (not, be)

Ⓑ 다음 괄호에 주어진 말을 이용하여 대화를 완성하시오.

1 A: _____ (let, close, the door)

　B: Yes, let's. It's too noisy outside.

2 A: _____ (let, order, some pizza)

　B: Yes, let's do that. I'm hungry.

3 A: _____ (let, play, a board game)

　B: No, let's not. I have a lot of work to do.

Ⓒ 다음 우리말과 일치하도록 괄호에 주어진 말을 배열하여 영작하시오.

1 밖에 너무 오래 있지 말자. (stay, not, outside, let's, too long)

　→ _____

2 우리 산책할까? (go, we, shall, for a walk)

　→ _____

3 우리 점심 같이 먹을까? (we, don't, together, why, eat, lunch)

　→ _____

4 도서관에서 공부할까? (about, studying, how, in the library)

　→ _____

5 모퉁이를 돌면 우체국이 보일 거야. (find, go, you'll, around the corner, and, the post office)

　→ _____

6 싸움을 멈추세요, 그렇지 않으면 경찰을 부를 거예요. (or, fighting, the police, stop, call, will, I)

　→ _____

WORKBOOK
Lesson 2

A 다음 주어진 문장을 what 감탄문으로 다시 쓰시오.

1 It is a very small animal.

→ _____

2 It is very exciting news.

→ _____

3 They are very old buildings.

→ _____

4 She has very long hair.

→ _____

B 다음 주어진 문장을 how 감탄문으로 다시 쓰시오.

1 The baby is very cute.

→ _____

2 The class was really boring.

→ _____

3 She sings very beautifully.

→ _____

4 You cook very well.

→ _____

C 다음 우리말과 일치하도록 괄호에 주어진 말을 배열하여 영작하시오.

1 그들은 정말 똑똑하구나! (how, they, smart, are)

→ _____

2 이 과제는 참 어렵구나! (how, this project is, difficult)

→ _____

3 당신은 정말 훌륭한 의사이군요! (what, a, doctor, you, good, are)

→ _____

4 그는 정말 아름다운 집을 가졌네요! (a, what, he, house, beautiful, has)

→ _____

5 그 거북이들은 참 느리게 움직이는 구나! (move, how, the turtles, slowly)

→ _____

A 다음 빈칸에 적절한 부가의문문을 쓰시오.

1 Mark is a cute boy, _____ _____?

2 You aren't going to buy new pants, _____ _____?

3 Jenny and Tom can't swim, _____ _____?

4 Mary enjoys cycling, _____ _____?

5 This novel is great, _____ _____?

B 다음 우리말과 일치하도록 괄호에 주어진 말을 배열하여 영작하시오.

1 화장실 좀 청소해라, 알았지? (will, the bathroom, clean, you)

→ _____

2 너는 회의에 없었어, 그렇지? (were, you, at the meeting, weren't, you)

→ _____

3 그들은 시험에 합격할 수 있어, 그렇지 않니? (can't, can, pass, they, the test, they)

→ _____

4 너는 노래를 잘 못해. 그렇지 않니? (very, don't, you, well, do, sing, you)

→ _____

5 우리 버스 정류장에서 만나자, 괜찮지? (shall, let's, meet, at the bus stop, we)

→ _____

6 그는 새로 산 휴대전화를 잃어버렸어, 그렇지? (he, lost, he, didn't, his new cell phone)

→ _____

C 다음 대화문의 ⓐ~ⓒ에 들어갈 알맞은 부가의문문을 쓰시오.

A: It is raining, ⓐ _____?

B: Yeah, it's raining really hard. Let's not go out today, ⓑ _____?

A: Wait. Tomorrow is Hailey's birthday. Did you buy a present for her?

B: Of course, I did. You didn't buy one, ⓒ _____?

A: No, I didn't. Oh, I have to go out to buy a present!

A 다음 〈보기〉에서 알맞은 의문사를 골라 대화를 완성하시오.

> 보기   who   why   where   what   when

1 A: _____ does your father do?

   B: He teaches math.

2 A: _____ does the plane arrive?

   B: At 10.

3 A: _____ is your brother?

   B: He is in the garden.

4 A: _____ is the girl with glasses?

   B: She is my niece.

5 A: _____ were you late?

   B: I was late because I missed the bus.

B 「How + 형용사/부사」를 이용하여 다음 대화를 완성하시오.

1 A: _____ pens do you have?   B: Twenty pens.

2 A: _____ is your sister?   B: She's 166 centimeters tall.

3 A: _____ do you go shopping?   B: Once a month.

4 A: _____ is your uncle?   B: He's 45 years old.

5 A: _____ is the backpack?   B: It's 50,000 won.

C 다음 우리말과 일치하도록 괄호에 주어진 말을 이용하여 문장을 완성하시오.

1 너는 아침에 누구를 만날 거니? (will, meet)

   → _____ in the morning?

2 너는 테니스와 배드민턴 중에서 어느 것이 더 좋니? (like)

   → _____ better, tennis or badminton?

3 그는 지금 무슨 과목을 공부하고 있니? (subject, study)

   → _____ now?

4 너의 아버지께서는 어떻게 너의 컴퓨터를 고치셨니? (your father, fix)

   → _____ your computer?

A 다음 〈보기〉에서 알맞은 접속사를 골라 문장을 완성하시오. (한 번씩만 쓸 것)

보기   or   so   but   and

1 Which do your parents want to do, hiking _____ golfing?

2 Anna can play soccer _____ baseball.

3 Sam can read Korean, _____ he can't understand it.

4 We were very hungry, _____ we went to the restaurant.

B 다음 밑줄 친 부분과 대등한 역할을 하는 것을 찾아 동그라미 치시오.

1 They went to the zoo, but they didn't see the pandas.

2 Mark and Julie are from England.

3 Richard loves music, so he wants to be a songwriter.

4 This bike is very cheap but really fast.

5 My dad likes doing the laundry and cleaning the bathroom.

6 Did you go fishing, or were you at the library?

C 다음 우리말과 같은 뜻이 되도록 주어진 단어를 배열하시오.

1 Carl은 많은 책을 갖고 있지만 그는 읽는 것을 좋아하지 않는다. (doesn't, he, them, but, reading, like)
   → Carl has many books, _____.

2 이 야채 주스는 맛있고 건강에 좋다. (delicious, is, vegetable juice, healthy, and, this)
   → _____

3 그들은 의사니 간호사니? (nurses, doctors, they, or, are)
   → _____

4 바람이 불고 비가 와서 우리는 집에 있었다. (home, so, stayed, we, at)
   → It was windy and rainy, _____.

5 나의 선생님은 영어, 독일어 그리고 프랑스를 하신다. (French, English, German, speaks, and, my teacher)
   → _____

A 다음 괄호 안에서 가장 자연스러운 것을 고르시오.

1 (Because/After/Before) we didn't have money, we couldn't watch the movie.

2 Be careful (because/when/after) you cross the street.

3 (Before/After/When) I blew out the candles, we ate the cake.

4 Please give me a call (before/because/after) you come to visit me.

B 다음 우리말과 같은 뜻이 되도록 알맞은 접속사를 써넣으시오.

1 너는 운동을 한 후에 샤워를 해야 해.

→ You should take a shower _____ you exercise.

2 해가 지기 전에는 날은 밝다.

→ It is bright _____ the sun goes down.

3 Jacob은 몸이 좋지 않아서 점심을 걸렀다.

→ Jacob skipped lunch _____ he wasn't feeling good.

4 왜 날 봤을 때 미소를 지었니?

→ Why did you smile _____ you saw me?

C 다음 〈보기〉에 주어진 말을 이용하여 ⓐ∼ⓓ를 채우시오.

보기	before	after	because	when

Ben: Meg. Do you want to go for ice cream ⓐ _____ we finish our homework?

Meg: Okay. By the way, I heard you joined the book club.

Ben: That's right.

Meg: How do you like it?

Ben: I really love the book club ⓑ _____ I can read great books and talk about them with the members.

Meg: Sounds fun. What club were you in ⓒ _____ you joined the book club?

Ben: I was in the hip-hop dance club.

Meg: Oh, right. You were dancing on the stage ⓓ _____ I saw you for the first time.

Ben: Yeah. I had so much fun in the club.

A 다음 밑줄 친 부분을 어법에 맞게 고쳐 쓰시오.

1 Sophie has a piano lesson <u>in</u> Sunday. → _____

2 We should meet <u>in</u> Saturday evening. → _____

3 The kids go to bed <u>on</u> midnight. → _____

4 I don't like the heat <u>on</u> summer. → _____

5 They are going to graduate from middle school <u>at</u> 2020. → _____

6 Many people are happy <u>at</u> Christmas Day. → _____

B 다음 주어진 단어로 빈칸을 채우시오.

보기　　　　　　until　　　during　　　for　　　by

1 The singer will sing _____ thirty minutes.

2 He played the video game _____ nine.

3 You should finish your homework _____ tomorrow.

4 We will travel in Spain _____ summer vacation.

C 다음 우리말과 같은 뜻이 되도록 주어진 단어를 배열하시오.

1 나는 2년 동안 캐나다에서 살 것이다. (two years, in Canada, live, I, for, will)

→ _____

2 나의 생일은 3월에 있다. (in, my birthday, March, is)

→ _____

3 점심시간은 정오에 시작합니다. (noon, begins, the lunch break, at)

→ _____

4 사람들은 4월 5일에 나무를 심는다. (on, trees, plant, people, April 5th)

→ _____

5 그들은 8시까지 공항에 도착해야 한다. (they, the airport, get to, should, 8, by)

→ _____

6 우리는 일출까지 해변에 머물렀다. (stayed, we, sunrise, at the beach, until)

→ _____

A 다음 두 문장에 공통으로 들어갈 알맞은 전치사를 써넣으시오.

1 • Tom grew up _____ a big city.
  • Jack was _____ Toronto during the holiday.

2 • We are going to meet her _____ the bus stop.
  • I'm planning to stay _____ home tomorrow.

3 • The artist put her paintings _____ the wall.
  • The student is sitting _____ the chair.

B 다음 우리말과 같은 뜻이 되도록 주어진 단어를 이용하여 문장을 완성하시오.

1 그는 등 뒤에 무엇을 숨기고 있지? (his back)
  → What is he hiding _____ _____ _____?

2 그 새끼강아지는 의자 아래서 자고 있다. (the chair)
  → The puppy is sleeping _____ _____ _____.

3 창문 위에 있는 시계는 너무 크다. (the window)
  → The clock _____ _____ _____ is too large.

4 나는 책장 옆에 전등을 하나 놓았다. (the bookshelf)
  → I put a lamp _____ _____ _____.

5 두 개의 벤치 사이에 오래된 나무 한 그루가 있다. (the two benches)
  → There is an old tree _____ _____ _____ _____.

C 다음 그림에 알맞게 대화문을 완성하시오.

James: Hello, Sue. I forgot to pack my book, glasses, and cell phone. Could you bring them to me?

Sue: Sure, where are they?

James: Can you see the laptop computer? The book is ⓐ _____ _____ it.

Sue: Oh, I got it. Where are the glasses?

James: They are ⓑ _____ _____ _____ the laptop computer, but I am not sure about the cell phone.

Sue: Your cell phone... Oh, it's ⓒ _____ the bookshelf.

James: Right, I left it there last night. Thank you.

Sue: You're welcome. I'll bring them to you soon.